Mies van der Rohe
The Krefeld Villas

Mies van der Rohe
The Krefeld Villas

Kent Kleinman and Leslie Van Duzer

Princeton Architectural Press, New York

For our parents

Published by

Princeton Architectural Press

37 East Seventh Street

New York, New York 10003

For a free catalog of books, call 1.800.722.6657.

Visit our web site at www.papress.com.

Editing: Scott Tennent

Design: Jan Haux

Special thanks to: Nettie Aljian, Dorothy Ball, Nicola
Bednarek, Janet Behning, Megan Carey, Penny (Yuen
Pik) Chu, Russell Fernandez, Clare Jacobson, John King,
Mark Lamster, Nancy Eklund Later, Linda Lee, John
McGill, Katharine Myers, Lauren Nelson, Molly Rouzie,
Jane Sheinman, Jennifer Thompson, Joseph Weston,
and Deb Wood of Princeton Architectural Press
—Kevin C. Lippert, publisher

Library of Congress Cataloging-in-Publication Data

Kleinman, Kent, 1956–

Mies van der Rohe : the Krefeld villas / Kent Kleinman
and Leslie Van Duzer.

p. cm.

Includes bibliographical references.

ISBN 1-56898-503-7 (alk. paper)

1. Museum Haus Lange Krefeld. 2. Museum Haus
Esters. 3. Architecture, Domestic—Germany—Krefeld.
4. Architecture—Germany—Krefeld—20th century.
5. Mies van der Rohe, Ludwig, 1886–1969—Criticism
and interpretation. 6. Krefeld (Germany)—Buildings,
structures, etc. I. Van Duzer, Leslie, 1958–
II. Mies van der Rohe, Ludwig, 1886–1969. III. Title.

NA7593.K74L54 2005

728.8'092—dc22

2004025603

Contents

Acknowledgments

Throughout the years, many people have lent their support to this project. First, and foremost, we have been graced with the patient and generous assistance of the Krefelder Kunstmuseen, administrator of Museum Haus Lange and Museum Haus Esters. Were it not for the early encouragement of Dr. Julian Heynen, former director of exhibitions and vice-director of the museums, we would not have pursued this project. His sustained investment in this undertaking proved invaluable, affording us the opportunity to dwell in the artist-in-residence apartments in Haus Esters—not once, but twice—and to freely access the villas and critical documents in the museum archive. We extend our appreciation to the museum's current director, Dr. Martin Hentschel, for his continuing support. To Volker Döhne, the museum staff photographer whose beautiful and haunting images of the villas populate this publication, words cannot adequately express our gratitude for more than a decade of generous offerings, expert advice, unexpected hospitality, and enduring friendship.

Our appreciation goes as well to Terence Riley, director of the Department of Architecture and Design at the Museum of Modern Art for granting us full access to the Mies van der Rohe Archive, and to Pierre Adler for his assistance in navigating the archive's extensive holdings.

To the Lange and Esters families, we owe our gratitude for graciously revealing their private family albums and permitting us an intimate glimpse into life in the villas. These photographs are reproduced here with the kind permission of Dr. Alfred and Lilo Krech and son Dr. Helmut Krech, Werner Lange and daughter Christiane Lange, and Joachim C. Heitmann.

We are grateful as well to all the artists who generously allowed us to reproduce their work. We offer our special thanks to Michael Asher who most kindly prepared an elaborated description of his installation. To Mies scholar Werner Blaser go our thanks for his permission to publish his drawings.

The research for this book was supported by an Arnold W. Brunner Grant. We are most appreciative of the New York Chapter of the American Institue of Architects for establishing this munificent award, without which this publication would likely not have been realized. Additional logistic support was generously provided by the University of Michigan and Arizona State University.

Our students from the University of Michigan, Arizona State University, and the State University of New York at Buffalo prepared the drawings for this publication and the elaborate structural models of the villas that have been exhibited internationally. Our thanks go to David Stockwell, Christian Unverzagt, Jeffrey Kershaw, Chad Schwartz, and Nobo Inoue for their dedication and precise work.

We offer Kevin Lippert and Clare Jacobson at Princeton Architectural Press our appreciation for trusting in us once again. It has been a true pleasure working with our editor, Scott Tennent, who has been thorough, perceptive, gentle but demanding, and always professional. His keen suggestions made a significant contribution to the final shaping of this text.

Finally, for their critical review of the manuscript and their insightful comments, we would like especially to thank Nancy Bartlett and Lisa Pincus. And to all our other friends and colleagues who believed our decade-long promise, we hope that this publication will reward your patience.

Introduction
Notes on Almost Nothing

Haus Lange and Haus Esters did not make Mies van der Rohe famous. One might even say that the two neighboring brick villas in Krefeld, Germany (1927–30) have long been treated as a threat to Mies's legacy: doubly damning evidence first repressed by the architect himself and subsequently suppressed by his apologists. The history of this neglect is in its own right revealing, for to make two substantial buildings essentially disappear suggests a remarkable degree of consensus between the architect and his critics. [2, 3]

Mies, as we know, said little about much, but particularly little was said about Haus Lange and Haus Esters. The architect proffered his only known assessment of the villas in a public dialogue at the Architectural Association in 1959. With thirty years of hindsight, Mies made his fateful condemnation: "I wanted to make this house [Haus Lange] much more in glass, but the client did not like that. I had great trouble."[1] This single remark—often published in tandem with an early pastel sketch of Haus Esters depicting a generously glazed garden facade or a photograph of the architect at work on the same—has been repeatedly cited to explain away these "compromised" works as the result of difficult clients. [1] Biographer Franz Schulze employs this coupling, suggesting as others before him that Haus Esters "might have been more impressive than it is if Mies had persisted with his concept of almost completely glazed running walls on the garden facade instead of keeping the windows discrete.... When the houses were finally built, these forward-looking inventions were abandoned, even, we presume from Mies's own recall, proscribed."[2]

[1]   Mies van der Rohe, early pastel sketch of Haus Esters

[1]

Curiously, during Mies's lifetime Haus Lange and Haus Esters were never exhibited as an ensemble; in fact, Haus Esters was never exhibited at all. Mies granted permission for the display of Haus Lange only twice, both times to his enthusiastic promoter, Philip C. Johnson, then director of the Department of Architecture and Design at the Museum of Modern Art.[3] In the catalogue for the 1947 Mies retrospective, Johnson describes both Krefeld villas as "badly damaged."[4] [4, 5] While Johnson's description of Haus Lange is fairly accurate—the villa sustained superficial damage from a parachute mine in 1943—there is no evidence to substantiate his claim concerning Haus Esters.[5] In contrast to this overstatement, Johnson lists Haus Wolf, Mies's other brick villa of the same period, in the same catalogue without any such qualifiers, despite its near total destruction during the war.[6] One is left to wonder if Johnson's description was calculated to divert the attention of future critics away from the Krefeld villas.

Whether an intentional slight or simply an oversight, Mies scholars took Johnson's cue well. A survey of early Mies monographs reveals an aggregated effort to downplay the importance—and in some cases existence—of these two buildings. In his 1955 monograph, Max Bill repeats Johnson's story, listing both Haus Esters and Haus Lange in the *Opere eseguite* as "molto danneggiata," despite the fact that Lange had since been restored.[7] One year later, Ludwig Hilberseimer omits any mention of the two villas altogether, and in 1964 Peter Blake describes the villas in passing as "several brick-and-glass villas for wealthy businessmen."[8] If one were to survey Werner Blaser's 1965 monograph, one would be left with the inaccurate impression that between 1924 and 1929 Mies designed nothing at all.[9]

The first significant treatment of the Krefeld villas was Wolf Tegethoff's 1981 landmark study of Mies's villas and country houses, an elaborate catalogue accompanying the first significant Mies exhibition following the founding of the Mies van der Rohe Archive at the Museum of Modern Art.[10] Tegethoff's thorough organization of the new archive made it difficult for scholars to ignore Haus Lange and Haus Esters. Surprisingly, however, subsequent Mies monographs were still remarkably scant in their coverage of the villas. In 1985 Franz Schulze's exhaustive biography dedicates a scarce two pages (four including photographs) to the Krefeld villas. In the same year, David Spaeth offers little more, praising them as "clear and sensitive," while criticizing their "almost conventional quality" and lack of "spatial excitement."

[2]   Haus Esters, east facade with laundry court

[3]   Haus Lange, northeast corner

[4]   Haus Lange, war damage to northeast corner, 1943

[5]   Haus Lange, war damage to upstairs bedroom corridor, 1943

[2]

[3]

[4]

[5]

Neither Academy Edition's 1986 *Mies van der Rohe: European Works*, nor Jean-Louis Cohen's 1994 *Mies Van der Rohe* grant the houses more than cursory mentions.[11]

In 1995, Kenneth Frampton's essay "Mies van der Rohe: Avant-Garde and Continuity" helped salvage Haus Lange and Haus Esters from obscurity by attempting to locate them along a continuous line of tectonic development compatible with, and pointing to, Mies's iconic works.[12] In the same year, Julian Heynen, director of exhibitions at the Kaiser Wilhelm Museum, edited the first dedicated monograph on the Krefeld villas. *Ein Ort für Kunst/A Place for Art* documents the history of the villas and provides the most extensive physical description of the buildings to date.[13] A second book by Heynen, published on the occasion of the reopening of the restored villas in 2000, *Ein Ort der denkt/A Place that Thinks,* largely repeats the text of the first but adds commentaries by numerous artists and meticulous photographs by museum staff photographer, Volker Döhne.[14] Most recently, Terence Riley and Barry Bergdoll presented the Krefeld villas for the first time on an even footing with Mies's other work in the 2001 Museum of Modern Art retrospective, Mies in Berlin.[15]

In spite of the recent publications and fanfare surrounding the restoration of the villas—and most surprisingly, in spite of the fact that the buildings have been accessible to the public for decades—Haus Lange and Haus Esters have rarely been treated critically, and never very extensively. This might in part be explained as the natural effect of major works on minor works. The brick villas, after all, lie in the double shadow of Mies's two contemporaneous masterworks: the German Pavilion (1929) and Villa Tugendhat (1930). This proximity is troubling, for it challenges the basic logic of an impressive historiographical project called "Mies." The shape of Mies's critical history—for histories, like sculpture, have form—is usually posited as a graceful, logarithmic curve with a steep trajectory at the self-defined beginning of his career, a slight flattening in the early 1930s, and from 1938 onward, a progressively decreasing rate of change, incremental advances becoming ever smaller. What has made this graph attractive and powerful as an organizing structure is the embedded logic of steady teleological progress, of a limited set of variables, of commitment to a single path, of consistency, of patience, of a destiny uninflected by minor quotidian contingencies or major cultural upheavals. It is a trajectory unique to Mies. All of the major (and most of the minor) projects have a place on this trajectory due to their commitment to a cluster of all-too-familiar Miesian formulas:

material discipline, tectonic integrity, structural clarity, spatial fluidity, and geometric simplicity.

With Haus Lange and Haus Esters, however, any number of well-worn Miesian formulas appear to be blatantly dysfunctional. The villas do not, for example, pick up the line of spatial invention initiated by their materially related forbearer, the Brick Country House, and they cannot be said, as both Tegethoff and Frampton have suggested, to lie midway on the path toward the typological maturation of the columnar pavilion. Far from Frampton's claim that "they were as formed by traditional constructional methods as they were influenced by avant-gardist spatial concepts,"[16] one must, in fact, state the opposite: the villas were formed by technical gymnastics in the service of rather traditional spatial concepts. The villas are also monumental evidence against the tectonic determinism offered by Werner Blaser, wherein the logic of the unitary brick module is held to permeate all formal moves.[17] Even the myth of the architect's uncompromising bearing is challenged by the story of Haus Lange and Haus Esters.

Goethe famously wrote "*Individuum est ineffabile*"–individuality is inexpressible–to which the art historian E. H. Gombrich has added *individuum est inexplicabile.*[18] Perhaps these two villas are excessively individuated–simply inexplicable, at least in conventional Miesian terms. But an important event in 1985 makes us think otherwise. The reconstruction of the German Pavilion in Barcelona produced an upheaval in Miesian scholarship, providing an occasion and a necessity for rereading Mies, as one could not engage that structure without confronting the fact that the defining terms that upheld the Mies canon were, if not inappropriate, at least inadequate. Structural clarity, geometric purity, formal autonomy, simplicity, even transparency–all dissipated in "attenuated smears of light," as Robin Evans described his experience of the pavilion's principal claim to rationality, namely its structural grid.[19] As many scholars grappled with the reconstructed pavilion, the criteria for assessing Mies's work shifted toward more complex, more embodied interpretations–readings that celebrated rather than denied the almost systematic negation of any rational method in Mies's work (if systematic negation of rationality is not itself a Miesian paradox).[20] In other words, the Mies trajectory is being replotted. In this context, Haus Lange and Haus Esters come ever more clearly into focus, for if any of Mies's works provide coordinates for a revised assessment and an expanded history, surely it is these two villas.

* * *

Haus Lange and Haus Esters have been portrayed as a single architectural ensemble, but Mies's relationships with Hermann Lange and Josef Esters cannot be viewed similarly as one. [6, 7] The difference between the two lifelong friends and business partners might best be described as the difference between a client and a patron. Absent any particular passion for the aesthetic battles of his day, Josef Esters was a client, one served by an architect recommended by a friend. By contrast, Hermann Lange—an active member of the Deutsche Werkbund, a major collector of modern art, and a well-connected representative of the German government—emerged from the Krefeld engagement as a patron, one who deliberately sought out his architect and promoted him loyally and repeatedly.

In 1886, at the age of 12, Hermann Lange moved to Krefeld, a major textile center close to the Dutch border, where his father, a silk manufacturer, founded several mills.[21] In 1919 he assumed control of his father's company, C. Lange Seidenwarenfabrik, and within a year formed a consortium of well-established Krefeld textile factories called the Vereinigte Seidenwebereien A.G. (United Silk Weaving Mills, Ltd.), or Verseidag. From its inception, Lange was the chairman of the board of Verseidag; his lifelong friend, Josef Esters, was a board member. This major entrepreneurial landmark was the foundation of Hermann Lange's fortune.

As an enterprising businessman and a highly visible advocate of the German textile industry, Lange played a leading role in the federal government. As early as 1917, during the final years of the First World War, he provided leadership in the Department of Raw Materials in the War Ministry, and a year later, headed a textile-related section of the Finance Ministry. After the war, as a director of the Imperial Finance Ministry, he was largely responsible for the peacetime conversion of the entire German textile industry. Lange continued to lend his services to the German State apparatus at the beginning of the Second World War, moving from Krefeld to Berlin to oversee the centralized distribution of textile goods. At his death in 1942, Lange was active on behalf of the National Socialist regime.

Lange was an early and aggressive proponent of the effort to unite art and industry as a strategy for forging a national identity for the nascent German nation. Historian Francesco Dal Co summed up this project succinctly: "To turn beauty, quality, and an aesthetic pursuit aimed at defending the solidest traditional values into cogwheels of an activity at once moral and political, to transform all this into

[6]   Hermann Lange
[7]   Josef Esters

[6]

[7]

compatible and useful instruments for a vast national enterprise of power—this was the goal."[22] In this spirit, as early as 1901, father Carl and son Hermann took up contact with leaders of the *Kunstgewerbebewegung*, the German arts and crafts movement, and commissioned designers Richard Riemerschmidt, Walter Leistikow and Peter Behrens to produce patterns for a new line, *Künstlerseide* (Artists' Silks). The role of the Krefeld-based Kaiser Wilhelm Museum and its founding director, Friedrich Deneken, was by no means peripheral to this union of art and industry. Indeed, the tight relationship between industry, the applied arts, and cultural institutions was in many ways itself inspired by the heated discourse on the question of national identity. It was Deneken who, in August 1900, instituted the first German Day of the Tailor exhibition, hosted by the Kaiser Wilhelm Museum, which was framed as a frontal attack on French fashion mongers whose imports were held responsible for corseting the German female into a state of potential infertility. The Krefeld museum was understood as a catalyst in the education of the textile industrialists that constituted its immediate support base; the industrialists, in turn, understood the museum as a vehicle for educating their customers; and the applied artists understood both the museum and the industrialists as collaborators in a grab for national attention and influence. This mutually supportive triad was augmented and formalized in Krefeld with the founding of the Krefelder Fachgruppe im Werkbund and the opening of an exhibition in 1911. Three years later Deneken hosted a major solo show of Werkbund cofounder, Hermann Muthesius, and a year after the war, organized a third exhibition of Werkbund work.

We should understand Hermann Lange in the context of this milieu. A Werkbund member himself, his boosterism on behalf of the Krefelder (and the greater German) textile industry was in equal measure a business strategy and a cultural mission. For Lange was not only one of Germany's most powerful industrialists, he was also one of Europe's foremost collectors of modern art; his frequent trips to Paris and Berlin were as much for the acquisition of art as they were for business. He began collecting in 1912 and, at the completion of the Krefeld villas in 1930, his collection numbered over 300 works by artists of international renown, including Picasso, Gris, Braque, Barlach, Belling, de Chirico, Marc, Maillol, Beckmann, Klee, Kokoschka, Nolde, Heckel, Müller, Kandinsky, Dix, Kirchner, Lembruck, and Leger.

How Hermann Lange first met Mies is unclear. According to Franz Schulze, who defers to Wolf Tegethoff, who refers to Sandra Honey, the introduction might have been made by Mies's associate, Lilly Reich: "the ladies [Frau Lange and Frau Esters] were clients at her couture salon, and the gentlemen had visited her small silk exhibition, designed in collaboration with Mies van der Rohe in 1926. There, in Frankfurt, they met Mies." It is also possible, according to Tegethoff, that Lange became acquainted with Mies through his connections to representatives of the modern movement in Berlin, or via a recommendation from Deneken, who was well connected to Mies's former employer Peter Behrens, or through contact with August Hoff, president of the Duisberg Museum Society where Mies exhibited in 1925.[23] Jan Maruhn and Nina Senger weigh in with the very plausible possibility that the two men met as members of the German Werkbund in 1926, the year Mies became vice president of the association.[24]

Regardless of how they met, Lange became a major force in Mies's career. Capitalizing on his substantial influence in national trade organizations and the federal government, fully aware of advances in the visual arts, and drawing on his personal wealth, Lange garnered ten commissions for Mies between 1926 and 1938, six of them for sites in Krefeld. Of these ten—three exhibitions designed in collaboration with Reich, four residential designs (the two Krefeld villas among them), and three commercial projects—half were realized. The commissions included such significant works as the Samt und Seide exhibition in Berlin, the unbuilt designs for the Krefeld Golf Club (of which Lange was the president), the Verseidag Factory Buildings in Krefeld (Mies's only industrial structures), the unbuilt Verseidag Administration Headquarters in Krefeld, an apartment renovation for Lange's daughter Mildred Lange-Crous in Berlin-Südende, and the unbuilt house for Lange's son Ulrich in Krefeld. Historians converge on the belief that it was also Lange who brought Mies and Lilly Reich to the attention of Dr. Georg von Schnitzler, a Reich commissar responsible for Germany's contribution to the 1929 International Exhibition in Barcelona.[25]

Lange hired Mies for the design of his house following a failed effort to work with the inexperienced team of Theo van Doesburg and Cornelis van Eesteren. No drawings were produced by the Dutch team, although they did meet with Lange on his parcel in the northeastern part of Krefeld in 1925.[26] The site was part of a bucolic setting developed in the 1880s as a greenbelt garden suburb. Zoning prohibited tall fences, prescribed seven-meter front yard setbacks, allowed only freestanding houses or units with only one party wall, and mandated single-use occupancy. Much of the infrastructure for the new suburb was constructed on fill to overcome the high-water table. In 1921 Lange purchased his 85-meter-wide-by-115-meter-deep lot for 105,000 marks. Two years later, Esters purchased the adjacent 75-by-115-meter lot for 950,000 marks, the disparity in land value a symptom of the rampant inflation that characterized the early Weimar years.[27] Mies was engaged by Hermann Lange and Josef Esters to design their neighboring villas on the Wilhelmshofallee in late 1927 or early 1928. [8, 9, 10] The structures were enclosed during the summer of 1929, and the Langes and Esters moved into the brick villas in the summer of 1930. [11]

Eight years later, Lange moved to Berlin, taking up a position with the federal government and leaving the villa in the care of his son Ulrich. Both the Lange and the Esters families occupied their villas intermittently throughout the war, despite the heavy bombardment of the industrial city of Krefeld and the damage caused to Haus Lange in 1943. Period photographs depict the Lange villa with shattered windows and an interior strewn with debris, but with its structure substantially intact. Following the war, Haus Esters was occupied by British authorities from 1945 to 1956; Haus Lange was leased from 1948 as office space while the war damage was repaired. In 1954 Ulrich Lange offered the house rent-free to the director of the Kaiser Wilhelm Museum, Paul Wember, for the display of modern and contemporary art, and in November 1955, Museum Haus Lange was opened to the public. When the initial agreement expired in 1966, Ulrich Lange gifted the house to the city for continued use as a museum. Ten years later, following the death of Josef Esters and his wife, the Esters heirs sold their villa to the city. Haus Esters was restored and opened to the public as Museum Haus Esters in 1981.[28]

The unique and inspired adaptive reuse of the two villas as museums, and the prophetic curatorial ambitions of a succession of gifted directors, sponsored a remarkable legacy in which a veritable parade of significant contemporary artists actively worked in and on these two challenging modern edifices. To be sure, not all the artists addressed the architecture in equal measure; some are simply exhibitions of work done rather than working engagements. But many of the artists—Claes Oldenburg, Jannis Kounellis, Michael Asher, Daniel Buren, Sol LeWitt, Richard Long, Richard

[8]   Aerial view of Wilhelmshofallee with Haus Lange
      and Haus Esters, 1930
[9]   Sitework for Haus Esters
[10] Haus Esters under construction
[11] Dining on the south-facing garden terrace,
      Haus Esters

[8]

[9]

[10]

[11]

Serra, Yves Klein, Christo and Jeanne-Claude, and Jan Dibbetts among them—advanced the liberation of painting from the frame and sculpture from the pedestal as a programmatic imperative. [12] For these artists, the conception/production of an installation necessarily involved the conception/production of the architecture. Some of these artists have become closely identified with Mies's architectural disposition. In fact, the most popular moniker for Mies's architecture only gained currency in relation to Mies after its introduction in the mid-1960s in relation to the work of these artists; before Serra, LeWitt and Judd, Mies could not (and was not) called what he is now so often said to be: a minimalist.[29]

All of the factors above—the historical lack of scholarship on the houses, the current instability of the terms in which Mies's oeuvre is being theorized, the fact of Lange as a supportive patron rather than merely a troublesome client, the proximity of art and architecture in both the conception of the villas and the milieu in which they were commissioned, and the unusual circumstance of a recent history of artworks that forged a critical relationship to these buildings—have shaped our reading of Haus Lange and Hause Esters. Our goal is to show that these structures carry the full measure of Mies's complex modernity; that they demonstrate another mode of that paradoxical complexity rather than an inferior or compromised one; that they are an aesthetic transformation of masonry typology just as the German Pavilion was of (the then hardly new) columnar typology; and that they are incorrectly read as transitional works rather than as a response to a specific program and a specific material. To be fair to history, the Krefeld villas do not expose their accomplishments casually, and what we celebrate as accomplishments were not always classified as such. But here we might draw a direct parallel to the recent reprocessing of Mies's iconic projects. After all, it has taken more than half a century for anyone to see the columns in the German Pavilion as "smears of light" rather than rationally deployed poles, and to earnestly consider the consequences of such a conception of structure.

To accomplish these goals we have adopted an atypical methodology. Each chapter views the architecture through the lens of an artist that has exhibited in Krefeld. We read the villas through their future history. Specifically, we leverage the installations of Yves Klein, Sol LeWitt, Richard Serra, and Ernst Caramelle to help dissect the mechanics of this architecture. In each case, the chosen artist forged a

[12] Christo wrapping the living room of Haus Lange, 1971

[12]

particular dialogue with Mies's architecture, and this dialogue constitutes serious analytic work. Klein's early installation curiously resuscitates the villa's original patterns of habitation; LeWitt's artistic practice sponsors a discussion of the role of process and instructions in Mies's architecture; Serra's anti-environmental installation forces a consideration of the anti-environment's environment; and Caramelle's paintings provide a perceptive spatial analysis of the architecture and a key clue to its techniques of destabilization.

This method has the advantage, but also the risk, of any surgical procedure in which portions of the body are covered to allow focused attention on a delimited site. The architectural analysis is circumscribed by the work of selected artists, and the discussion of the artists is concentrated on their work in the villas. This double bracketing of the subject allows an intensity of investigation not typical of either architectural or art historical monographs. Those interested in longitudinal studies of either the artists or the architect will find this topical approach unsatisfying, if not actually circumspect, for the intersection of artist and building is, to a degree, a contingent event. LeWitt's art was not invented when he drew on the walls of Haus Lange, and his practice did not change when he departed; nor, obviously, was the design of the villa informed by the various creative agendas of the artists, who entered the scene long after Mies had conceived of the architecture.

Although the method is unusual, it is not without provenance. From their inception, both Haus Esters and Haus Lange were designed to complete themselves with artworks; the artists that have exhibited in these buildings have thus participated in the original dialogue initiated by the clients. Josef Esters and Hermann Lange were not, programmatically speaking, blank slates. The architecture of the Krefeld villas was more constrained and less totalizing than was typical for much of Mies's work precisely because each client, but particularly Lange, demanded an architecture to house his art. Mies was required to work close to a conventional notion of dwelling in Krefeld, with rooms and doorways and windows and walls, and was prevented from sweeping such architectural conventions aside by radicalizing the definition of enclosure and totalizing the interior.

This circumstance has caused some to imagine that Mies either compromised excessively, or willingly subdued his avant-garde aspirations to please an important client. We believe in a third option, namely that Mies abandoned none of his critical

overleaf
[13]   Celebration on the terrace, Haus Esters

agenda but exercised his modernity at the scale of the room, the doorway, the window, the wall, the brick. The result is an architecture that is both normative and radical, one in which conventions are destabilized but not eradicated. In this sense, the buildings are nothing less than a meditation on the bricks and mortar of architecture.

Klein's kleine Kammer [1]

Mies usually had his way. He had a talent for either connecting with the ideal patron (Tugendhat), finding the degree zero program (Barcelona), dominating the client (Farnsworth), or knowing when to fold (Ulrich Lange project). Given free reign, Mies produced masterworks of such total coherence that they have become benchmarks both for the architect and for the entire modern movement in architecture. Assimilating the Krefeld villas into this legacy has been difficult, for it seems obvious that these commissions did not yield the conditions under which Mies produced his most renowned projects. Put bluntly, Mies's talent for constructing the ideal client seems to have failed him. He landed a job in which the contingencies of the program and the proclivities of the client were sufficiently weighty to withstand his (likely divided) attention.

But Mies did not fold, and instead invested more than two years working on Haus Esters and Haus Lange at exactly the same time that he was producing the German Pavilion and Villa Tugendhat. The standard explanation of the Krefeld villas is that they could and should have been the masterwork that ended up in Brno, but instead became, at best, curious transitional pieces limited by the nature of the commissions. This explanation has the distinct advantage of maintaining, at least in appearance, the coherence of Mies's architectural legacy, because it allows the Krefeld villas to be understood as modestly and harmlessly anomalous due to forces external to the architect's creative will. This explanation has a distinct disadvantage, however, in that it requires a massive suspension of disbelief, for it seems quite clear that Haus Lange and Haus Esters are programmatically, spatially, and structurally so distinct from either Farnsworth or Tugendhat as to be essentially different genres: the one could never become the other.

[1] Yves Klein in the Void Room, Museum Haus Lange, 1961

[1]

Nor are these two villas so singularly odd, for Mies designed a number of dwellings and galleries during the same time period for clients with heavy programmatic baggage—for example, the Erich Wolf House (1925–27), the Fuchs House addition (1928), and the Ernst Henke House (1930). None of these projects have entered into Mies's legacy with much force or critical attention. No photographs of the interiors of these projects were published by the architect, as if the sheer opacity of these works—or perhaps more specifically, their capacity to embrace a variety of domestic habits—excluded them from being truly modern exemplars. This exclusion has fueled sustained criticism aimed explicitly at modern architecture's ability to coexist with the quotidian habits of domesticity, beginning with Justus Bier's 1931 critique of the "livability" of Haus Tugendhat to Alice Friedman's similar critique of the Farnsworth House some seven decades later.[1] In this sense, the architect's own editorial hand has had a self-limiting effect on the range and relevancy of his legacy. Ironically, an argument favoring Mies's modernity as an instructive and durable model across a range of architectural circumstances—a position that characterizes this book—requires an argument against Mies's own self-construction.

History and circumstances have conspired to make Krefeld an appropriate site for launching such an argument, for the two villas had the temerity not only to have survived the war years essentially intact, but also to have entered public circulation as successful museum venues for many of the mid-twentieth century's most progressive artists, thereby receiving extensive exposure. The Krefeld villas are thus a kind of friction in the Mies machinery. What follows is the tale of two reactions to this friction. The first centers on the work of the artist Yves Klein who, in his installation at Haus Lange, unwittingly delighted in precisely that aspect of the architecture that has proven most troublesome for Mies scholars—namely, the conventional cellular nature of the plan. The second is the counter-reaction by the postwar stewards of both villas, who sought to overcome the friction by nudging them sufficiently close to the gravitational pull of the architect's mainstream identity.

Programmatically, the shift in 1955 from a private gallery for Hermann Lange's extensive art collection to that of a public museum for temporary exhibitions might seem subtle—merely a question of rehanging and relabeling. Initially, this was indeed the case. During the five years between 1955 and 1960, Haus Lange served the public much as it had served its former owner. Lange had insisted on ample wall space to display his sizable collection; rooms were discretely configured as chambers for art, including wall-mounted travertine pedestals intended for statuettes and ample unarticulated wall surfaces for paintings. The cellular nature of the plan yielded a series of *Kunstkabinette*, a spatial paradigm not unprecedented for this architect when faced with the challenge of housing an art collection. The early public exhibitions in Haus Lange reenacted the original relationship between art and architecture. In this relationship, the architecture assumed a background character and also a quality of incompleteness, as if the art—or more generally, habitation—was anticipated by the architecture and made whole by it. An image of the 1957 exhibition of the artist Käthe Kollwitz demonstrates the continuation of this relationship during the early years of the villa's public life. In fact, this image is a rare photograph of the Lange dining room in its original configuration, with a wood partition wall separating the dining room from the living room, thereby creating a fully enclosed interior space. [2]

The relatively neutral, almost conventional character of the villa's interior architecture may not fit our contemporary expectations of Mies's work, but it was celebrated at the time in the only published review of the villa. In 1931, in an article by the art critic Walter Cohen in the journal *Museum der Gegenwart* (*The Contemporary Museum*), the interior of Lange was explicitly praised as an exemplary piece of modern architecture precisely because it countered what Cohen called the "*Bilderfeindlichkeit der neueren Wohnarchitektur*"—the contention that modern architecture was hostile to art.[2] With obvious irony, Cohen cites Mies's own Weissenhofsiedlung in Stuttgart as the prime example of this undesirable "*Bilderfeindlichkeit*" (literally "picture-hostility"), to which Mies's own Haus Lange was the antithesis. Cohen praised the tranquil spaces of Haus Lange, the extensive white walls and occasional wood paneling, and the simple wall-mounted pedestals as an ideal, non-distracting, harmonious setting for Lange's collection of paintings and sculpture. *Bilderfeindlichkeit* was, of course, merely code for the larger criticism that much modern architecture was unreceptive to the habits and indelible to the traces of domestic life in general. All coded pretense would be dropped during the furor caused by Villa Tugendhat in 1931, in which the issue of *Bilderfeindlichkeit* was posited openly as a question of *Lebensfeindlichkeit* (life-hostility) because of the totalizing aesthetic program of Mies's Brno project. In short, Haus Lange (and Haus

Esters) were very different in program and principle from the works that would make and mark Mies's architectural identity.

In the same year that Haus Lange was opened to the public as a museum, a young Frenchman decided to abandon all hope of becoming the president of the French Judo Federation and instead dedicate his life to art. In 1955, at the Club de Solitaires in Paris, Yves Klein opened his first solo exhibition with a small showing of mono-chromatic canvases. Klein rapidly expanded his artistic program, creating entire genres of artwork in breathless succession. At a double exhibition at two Left Bank Parisian galleries in the late 1950s, Klein released 1001 blue balloons into the Parisian ether, creating the first *sculpture aerostatique*. He ignited sixteen firecrack-ers on a blue-painted panel that created, in the process of combustion, a one-minute artwork entitled *Feux de bengale/tableau de feu bleu d'une minute (Bengal Fire of One-Minute Blue Fire Painting)*. Between 1955 and 1960, he gravitated to projects distinctly architectural in scale. In 1958 he was awarded a commission to decorate the foyer of the new opera house in Gelsenkirchen, Germany. There he met architect Walter Ruhnau and began to align his artistic aspirations and theoretical proclama-tions with some of the era's most progressive architectural conceptions: lightweight fabric structures, pneumatic buildings, and an imagined architecture of "walls of fire,...walls of water, like the roofs of air" consisting of enclosures of pure air, pres-surized blasts that establish a weatherized interior, and fire and water fountains that would heat or cool entire urban areas—in short, an immaterial urbanity.[3] In 1957, Klein exhibited *Immaterial*, consisting of an empty gallery room in the Gallerie Collete Allendy; a year later, at the Gallerie Iris Clert, he presented a completely empty gallery space coated entirely—walls, curtains, cabinets—with white paint, entitled *Spécialisation de la sensibilité à l'état matière première (Specialization of Sensibility in the Raw Material State of Stabilized Pictorial Sensibility, the Void)*.

On February 3, 1960, the first director of Museum Haus Lange, Paul Wember, invited Klein to exhibit his work in the villa. Klein was enthusiastic about producing a comprehensive retrospective in what he called "Mies's fine work," although it is unlikely that the artist was as yet familiar with the building.[4] In a nine-page letter responding to Wember's invitation, Klein proposed an expansive exhibition/event program and asked the museum director to send him plans of the ground floor and

[2]   Käthe Kollwitz commemorative exhibition, Museum Haus Lange, 1957. Former dining room with original wood partition wall

[2]

the gardens of Haus Lange.[5] Klein visited the villa in the summer of 1960 and again in the late fall. He was encouraged by the architecture he discovered. The organization of the exhibition was captured on an annotated plan sketch produced by the artist. [3] The living room was to become a blue zone, hung with large blue monochromes. The former man's room became the equivalent in pink, the adjacent drawing room a zone of gold, the woman's room a zone of mixed works, and the dining room a second blue zone. At the entrance to the villa, Klein proposed a jet of fire, and to terminate the exhibition on the garden terrace, he conceived of two additional fire-works: a single fire-fountain and a fire-wall consisting of a matrix of fifty Bunsen burners. [4, 5] For the opening night, Klein proposed a performance of his twenty-minute, single-pitch monosymphony for twenty classically trained musicians. The performance was scuttled, however, due to protests from the concertmaster of the city's orchestra, who felt that the monotone piece was beneath his dignity.[6]

Despite the adventurous conception of the entire exhibition, Klein desired not an equally adventurous architecture, but rather a fairly conventional setting: a series of five chambers, a principal origin, and a distinct terminus. He made but two modest requests of the museum director regarding changes to the architecture. First, on the plan given to the artist by Wember, Klein inscribed the question: "is it possible to close here with a wall in a clean manner?"[7] and with a bold arrow, Klein indicated the location of the wall he had in mind, a separation between the former dining area and the living room. Second, Klein noted, "an empty room will have to be reserved for the specialization and atmospheric stabilization of my 'Void' volume of immaterial pictorial sensibility."[8] Deciphered, Klein wanted to produce a "void room" similar to that in the Gallerie Iris Clert two years earlier and was requesting an enclosed space independent of the main circulation. The appropriate location for Klein's void room was obvious to the artist and was clearly inscribed on his annotated floor plan as "*le Vide.*" The room identified by Klein was an existing, aberrant, windowless chamber. It is centrally located in the ground-floor plan yet is clearly marginal—if not actually destructive—to the plan's spatial organization. One Klein scholar described the space as a "room constructed arbitrarily after the war."[9]

Because of its marginal nature, the room was ideal for Klein's purposes, and the director concurred. Klein prepared the space personally, painting all six surfaces, and the doors, and the keys to the doors with IKI—International Klein Immaterial—a

[3]   Yves Klein, plan for *Monocrhome und Feuer* exhibition in Museum Haus Lange, 1960

[4]   Klein, fire-fountains collage, 1960

[5]   Fire-fountains installed at Museum Haus Lange, 1961

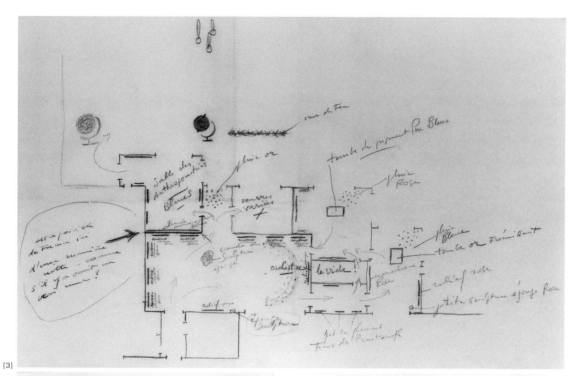

[3]

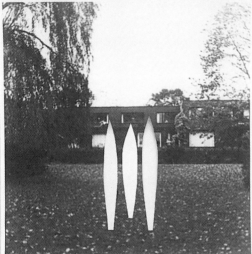

Musée de Krefeld (Ruhr)
Vue du fond de la Pelouse
sur le Musée intérieure.
Trois Flammes Flottantes respectives
3m, 3m50, 4m et diamètre 80cm

[4]

[5]

white paint mixed with a granular additive.[10] [6] A single fluorescent tube centered on the ceiling illuminated the volume. [7] At the close of Klein's exhibition, Wember and Klein convened in the "void room" and executed the transfer, from artist to director, of a "zone of pictorial immaterial sensibility."[11] As of February 26, 1961, Mies's Haus Lange became the material home to this immaterial work of Yves Klein. The room exists to this day in its Kleinian condition, and it holds a significant place in the history of mid-twentieth-century art as one of the earliest examples of installation art.[12] In Klein's legacy, the room is generally considered a singular and historic landmark; in both the art-historical and art-market sense of the term, *le Vide* is invaluable and, consequently, it is indestructible.

Despite Klein's radical practice he, arguably more than any other artist who exhibited in Haus Lange, exploited the inherent conservatism of the villa's spatial organization. Unwittingly perhaps, Klein, with his two modest architectural moves, also produced a tidy act of historic preservation with almost archeological precision. The divider that Klein desired between the dining room and the living room was precisely where Mies had originally provided a wood partition wall, a wall Wember had had removed shortly before Klein visited the villa. Wember's motive was ostensibly to enhance circulation through the gallery, but he was undoubtedly encouraged by the fact that modifying the original condition rendered the space more fluid and—in a word used here as a trope and not a signature—more "Miesian." Klein received his wall, but only temporarily, as it was permanently removed after his exhibition closed.

Klein's second act of preservation, however, was permanent, for the small, apparently arbitrary room which became *le Vide* only appears arbitrary. It dates from the original construction period between 1928 and 1930, and it was provided to Herr Lange by Mies himself. The chamber is absent from the August 1928 design drawings for Haus Lange, but is present in the as-built drawings produced by Mies in 1931. [8, 9] In other words, despite its evident disfiguring effect on the plan, it is, more or less, part of the original condition. The chamber was apparently a late programmatic demand by Herr Lange, who required a space to house an organ and its battery of pipes. The keyboard faced the living room and was framed within a large opening incorporated into the symmetrical composition of the living room's west wall, the chamber itself accessed by a small door from Lange's study. The organ was

[6]   Klein prepares the Void Room, 1961

[7]   The completed Void Room

[8]   Haus Lange, ground-floor plan without organ
      chamber, 1928

[9]   Haus Lange, as-built ground-floor plan with
      organ chamber, 1931

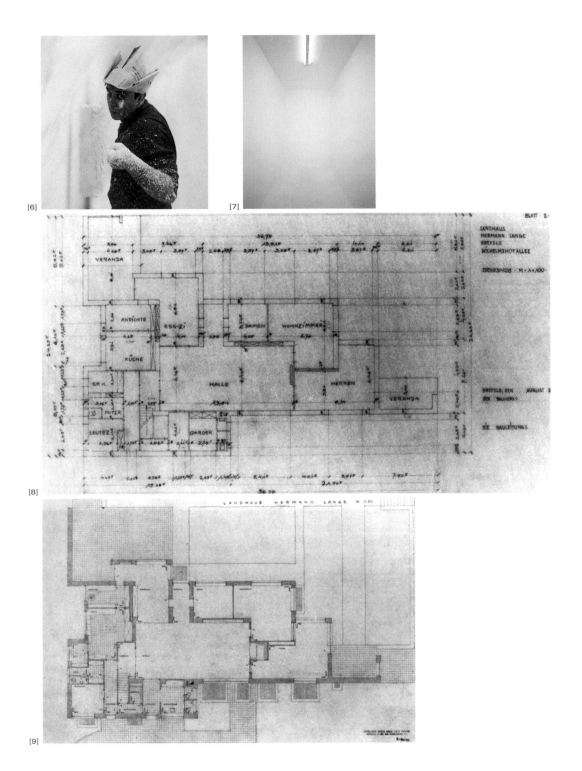

[6]

[7]

[8]

[9]

hidden behind a floor-to-ceiling curtain, which was drawn back to present the instrument as the principal theatrical focus of the room. [10] Shortly after the war, the chamber's opening to the living room was walled up and plastered over, thus "restoring" the western wall of the main room to an ontologically curious "pre-original" condition–that depicted in the construction drawings. During the same period, the organ chamber was enlarged, and a connecting door between the chamber and the drawing room was added. This is the condition that was presented in the plans sent to Klein, and this is the condition his intervention has since rendered immutable.

There is little doubt that both the dining room partition wall and the ill-resolved chamber distract from our image of Mies's architecture and persona. Mies's architecture is not supposed to have the compositional slack nor the architectural opacity necessary to absorb this kind of programmatic and spatial ballast, and Mies is known to have resisted when such slack was demanded. Yet Haus Lange does have slack and opacity. The now-missing partition wall and the little chamber for Lange's organ are but traces of an architecture that approached the contingencies of habitation and program not as obstacles, but as constructive parameters. This is not to imply that the architect embraced this modality enthusiastically; his self-constructed legacy certainly suggests otherwise. Rather, it is an attempt to recuperate a condition about which little has been said because these conditions have been expunged from the historical record. The chamber "discovered" by Klein is but a fragment of an entire interior milieu that has been deemed expendable from the history of this building and this architect. To find this authentic fragment embedded in a structure by Mies allows us to ponder what has been removed and why, to retrace what the whole might once have been, and to potentially celebrate an architecture, perhaps even an architectural movement, different from that which we have come to expect.

We might not expect, for example, that both Haus Esters and Haus Lange comfortably sheltered a fully bourgeois domestic environment. To be sure, in characteristic fashion, Mies had tried to extend aesthetic control over the interiors of both villas; he drew up several plans for both Haus Lange and Haus Esters that included chairs labeled "*Pavillion Sessel*," undoubtedly referring to the chairs he designed for the German Pavilion in 1929. [11] But these plans were never executed. Mies did produce furniture for the Esters and Lange dining rooms–exquisitely crafted chairs and tables that are stylistically modern but not technologically or materially

[10]   Haus Lange, living room with draped opening, 1931

[11]   One of several proposed furniture layouts for Haus Lange's living room

[10]

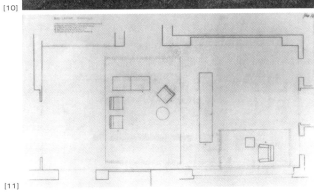

[11]

innovative, [12] but only in the woman's room in Haus Lange was Mies granted full control over the interior appointments. [13] For all the other rooms, the owners came with the domestic trappings of the upper-class bourgeoisie. Esters and Lange had their own furnishings, a vast array of Biedermeier items: carved vitrines, sofas, plump armchairs, lamps with pleated shades, desks with anatomical legs, floral carpets, lace doilies, and potted plants. [14, 15] The majority of the rooms in the Krefeld villas housed the very material culture that Mies emphatically and programmatically rejected. Indeed, the interiors of Lange and Esters as lived looked dangerously similar to the nineteenth-century interior illustrated on the famed poster for the 1927 Werkbund exhibition in Stuttgart, produced during Mies's tenure as Werkbund director, that depicted a dim and cluttered interior crossed out with a graffiti-like red "X" and covered with the words "wie wohnen?" ("how to dwell?"). [16, 17] With little effort one could imagine that despised nineteenth-century interior being the architect's own twentieth-century villa in Krefeld.

But why is this apparent similarity dangerous? Because it was understood, by Mies and his early biographers, that the architect's purported contribution to modern architecture could not be squared with anything short of a revolution in the culture of dwelling. The accommodation of what was clearly a robust bourgeois life by a purportedly modern architect was not only stylistically incongruous, but it jeopardized an entire architectural paradigm. At risk was the presumed organic relationship between life and its habitat, between modern architecture and modern culture. Mies's version of this paradigm is exemplified most forcefully and fully by Villa Tugendhat in Brno, designed and built almost contemporaneously with the Krefeld villas. Tugendhat represents the architect's most comprehensive transformation of the culture of dwelling, a thorough cleansing and a complete proposition for a transformed domesticity. The approach has been called minimal, but it is in fact the opposite: it is architectural maximalism, excess rather than dearth, yielding an entire ecology of dwelling rather than merely an architectural artifact. The delicate, almost undetectable architecture of slender columns and thin skins was an environment in which old habits had no oxygen. The plan was designed to accommodate a new population of inhabitants, both people and things. The scope of design extended to all scales and domains, including, of course, the furnishings. In Villa Tugendhat, the furniture was fully incorporated into the compositional strategy, and from the earliest sketches to

[12]   Haus Esters, dining room with Mies furniture
[13]   Frau Lange's room with Mies furniture
[14]   Herr Esters's room with original furniture
[15]   Herr Lange's room with original furniture

[12]

[13]

[14]

[15]

the final inked images prepared for publication, the furniture is depicted with remarkable precision and fixity. Over the entire course of the design development, these items undergo only the slightest displacements, and period photographs suggest that the blueprint for dwelling was followed faithfully during the brief period of occupation by Fritz and Grete Tugendhat. The furnishings are architectural fragments, subject to the spatial geometries of the plan and the material palette of the building. The sideboard is as much a freestanding wall as it is a storage unit as it is a miniature chromed columned reflective architectural body; the dining room table and chairs are pinned to the same center as the enclosing semicircular wall; even the grand piano is as much a circulation modulator as it is a musical instrument.

The assignment of such precise spatial and tectonic roles to what are normally independently conceived and acquired quotidian objects raises significantly the demands on such items far beyond that which they can bear. This is hardly accidental: the instrumental precision demanded of the furniture effectively eliminates the contingent and the happenstance, and much is disqualified by the method. Filling the resulting void, Mies designed over forty unique pieces of furniture for the Tugendhats, more than for any other domestic commission.[13] This extensive reach deep into the quotidian domestic sphere was the source of much praise and much condemnation. The two most experienced voices that have emerged from the interior of Mies's houses—those of Greta Tugendhat and Edith Farnsworth—represent extreme poles of the critical spectrum. The first produced some of the most supportive and enlightened testimony; the second, some of the most damning.[14] For Tugendhat this new ecology was uplifting, for Farnsworth it was oppressing. These differences notwithstanding, there was no disagreement that the totalized environment was integral to, and inextricable from, the architectural conception. The furniture completes the architecture. Consequences follow logically: a Mies interior without Mies furniture is an incomplete job, and a Mies interior that comfortably hosts a nineteenth-century armoire is not a Mies. Haus Lange and Haus Esters, which demonstrate a curious potential to be both modern and indifferent to their interior contents, have fared poorly under this logic.

In 1981 a unique opportunity arose in Krefeld to test this normative reasoning. In the late 1970s, the Esters family agreed to sell their villa to the city of Krefeld, placing an ensemble of significant Mies dwellings into public hands for the first

[16] Frau Esters's room with original furniture, 1930s
[17] Werkbundausstellung: *Die Wohnung*. Graphic by Willi Baumeister, 1927

[16]

[17]

time. Both villas were placed under the management of the Kaiser Wilhelm Museum to function as paired contemporary art galleries, and in 1981 Haus Esters joined Haus Lange as a public museum. It was a singular opportunity to redress the historical reception of the ensemble. With tactical brilliance, Paul Wember's successor as museum director, Gerhard Storck, conceived of an inaugural exhibition consisting of a comprehensive review of Mies's villas and country houses to be displayed in both Haus Esters and Haus Lange. The stage was set for positioning the Krefeld villas within a reconceived Miesian trajectory, with the two villas primed for the dual role as both site and subject of an exhibition whose goal was to challenge the received notion of Mies by showing the full range of his creative output. In doing so, space would naturally be made for Mies's lesser-known, anomalous works, even works that had been shunned by the architect himself—works like the two Krefeld villas.

In preparation for the exhibition, Storck approached the Museum of Modern Art in New York for material from the Mies van der Rohe Archive. Finding the material largely unprocessed, Mies scholar and exhibition co-curator, Wolf Tegethoff, began the task of archiving the Museum's holdings in 1979. Arthur Dexler, MoMA director of the Department of Architecture and Design, described Tegethoff's effort as the first major research project undertaken by an independent scholar working at the Mies archive.[15] Tegethoff's labors yielded a critical and comprehensive assessment of Mies's major domestic projects based on the archival, rather than the apocryphal, record. The resulting publication, *Mies van der Rohe: Villen und Landhausprojekte*, accompanied the Krefeld exhibition, and in 1985 the book was translated into English. It remains the principal catalogue raisonné of Mies's domestic projects. For Storck, there was no question that the legacy of Mies's modern architecture had been inappropriately distilled to a few overexposed works, and that this exhibition would function to problematize the prevailing reductive view of modernity with a number of very specific, underexposed counterexamples. In his foreword to Tegethoff's catalogue, Storck made his ambitions for the exhibition and the accompanying publication clear:

> The extent of his [Tegethoff's] study and its scholarly style may represent
> something of a barrier to some readers uninterested in penetrating so fully
> into the material; still it was essential to provide considerably more than

the usual picture book with its customary descriptions.... It was time to do away with the usual array of images that display everything in a unified style—not to keep this tradition alive with yet another collection of photos and general pronouncements. To demonstrate this need, one has but to step inside the Lange and Esters houses and experience for oneself that some things are quite different from what we have been led to believe.[16]

"Step inside": Storck's directive was an invitation to come to Krefeld to experience the villas firsthand. But to no less a degree it was a challenge to step into a new body of scholarship and images on the architect's oeuvre via Tegethoff's publication, for the "usual picture book with its customary descriptions" had, as Storck knew well, little interest in the Krefeld villas. The interiors of Haus Lange, and particularly Haus Esters, were essentially unpublished works. Two early images of the Lange interiors—the living room and the woman's room—had been included in Walter Cohen's 1931 article, but his piece focused primarily on Lange's renowned art collection, not on Mies's architecture. We know that Mies consented to having these two images published, as Cohen explicitly thanked the architect for his cooperation, but this was the first and last time that he would grant permission to publish images of the villa interiors.[17] Even in the 1932 Museum of Modern Art's Modern Architecture: International Exhibition—to which Hermann Lange was a financial contributor—and in the subsequent book *The International Style*, only exterior views of Haus Lange were presented.[18] Between the opening of Haus Lange to the public in 1955 and the exhibition by Storck in 1981, its interior was presented only as background in the context of ongoing art installations. The case of Haus Esters was even more extreme: no images of its interior were published at all prior to Storck's exhibition. Given this history of exclusion, Storck's invitation to "step inside" has the air of a circus barker proffering a marvelous revelation, cracking open the doors to a world where things are "quite different from what we have been led to believe." But what the public saw in person and in print in 1981—and continues to see in print to this day—was a decorous attempt to introduce the villas as legitimate creations of the master, and thus a reproachmont with modernity rather than a confrontation. The terms of this détente can be discerned with some clarity by reviewing three photographs taken around the time of the 1981 exhibition.

The first depicts the dining room of Haus Lange and was published as the only interior view of Haus Lange in Tegethoff's catalogue. [18] It depicts a spatially continuous, almost aqueous floor plane that begins from the middle background and spills off the bottom of the image. A similar spatial flow is implied from side to side as the reflective floor surface appears to continue behind a dark vertical band that reads like a pillar or column and divides the image asymmetrically. The large dining room window and the glazed door to the garden beyond appear as one continuous glazed plane. Occupying the former dining area, perched delicately on stainless steel legs, are two *Pavillion Sessel*, a matching ottoman, and the well-known "X" steel and glass table, all designed by Mies. By any measure, this photograph is an impressive creation, because the major thematic aspirations of the image are not merely unhistorical, but actively, coherently, and creatively so: Mies's iconic furniture was never part of the villa's interior; the glazed garden door and the dining room window do not lie in the same plane, but are in fact offset; and the dark vertical band is in fact the narrow face of a 50-centimeter-thick wall that firmly separates the former dining room from a discrete corridor. Indeed, the entire view would have been impossible if the original wall that separated the dining area from the living room were in place (the same wall, incidentally, requested by Klein). [19] In the words of Storck's colleague, Julian Heynen, the image is designed "to correspond to the architect's intentions more closely than what must in the end have been a compromise with the clients' needs."[19] This photograph has had an influential future, for as late as 2000 it was reproduced in a monograph on the architect in which it was suggested that the imported chairs were, in fact, a product of the Krefeld commission.[20]

A second representative photograph depicts the children's room of Haus Esters. [20] The signature furniture—two Barcelona chairs, a matching ottoman, and the Tugendhat coffee table—is again not authentic to the original condition. Notable is the spatial continuity across three originally discrete entities—the children's room, the corridor connecting the living room with the garden terrace, and Frau Lange's private room—a view made possible by removing two sets of double leaved doors. This image has also demonstrated considerable durability: it was initially published in Heynen's monograph, the first on the two villas, and reproduced in modified form without furniture in his subsequent monograph of 2000, and again, slightly cropped, in Yehuda Safran's Mies monograph of the same year.[21]

[18]   Museum Haus Lange, modified dining room, 1981
[19]   Käthe Kollwitz exhibition, Museum Haus Lange, same general view as [18], 1957.

[18]

[19]

[20]

[20] Museum Haus Esters, modified children's room,
1981
[21] Museum Haus Lange, man's room and the
adjacent drawing room without original dividing
bookcase
[22] Drawing of original bookcase

[21]

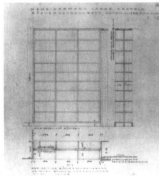

[22]

A third representative photograph is that of the staggered windows on the south facade of Haus Lange as seen from within the private study of Herr Lange. [21] Published in both of the existing monographs on the Krefeld houses, this view depicts the zigzagging exterior window wall that frames and captures the exterior like a pleated strip of film.[22] A continuous folded plane, the exterior wall is comprised of impressively large, utterly transparent glass panes joined by slender white plaster strips that function not as bearing points, but as mere hinges at the folds, forming a boundary independent of any interior partitions. The floor plane of oak herringbone parquet and the wood baseboards flow seamlessly between the staggered volumes, as does the white plaster ceiling; there are no thresholds and no headers. Here again, this remarkable architectural configuration is authentic only to the degree that it is a "clarification" of the original condition, skillfully rendered and bolstered by the same logic that has governed the contemporary representation, reconstruction, and reception of the villa. Mies had originally designed a floor-to-ceiling and wall-to-wall, two-sided wood bookcase that divided what were in fact two private chambers. [22] Herr Lange's study and the adjacent drawing room originally had no physical connection to one another.

Clearly, the guiding philosophy from at least 1981 onward was that the Krefeld villas could achieve an elevated state of originality and legitimacy, to the degree that they relinquish part of their actual history.[23] The specific parts that seemed expendable were those considered the product of the architect's "compromise" with the clients. Tegethoff articulated this stance with respect to the furniture in his catalogue text on the preparation of Haus Lange for the 1981 exhibition. "The loss of the original furnishings, which were kept by the former owners, is of no particular consequence, especially since there were scarcely any original pieces involved," wrote Tegethoff, assuming that these two modes of originality, and their respective value, needed no further explanation. Tegethoff continued: "Mies was given a free hand only in the furnishing of the ladies' sitting room of the Lange House; everywhere else he had to make do with existing pieces. It would, of course, be helpful if this room could be preserved as it was reconstructed for the 1981 exhibition."[24] Dismissing almost all of the original furnishings while archiving the single room in the entire villa complex furnished by the architect is evidence that a fairly selective filter was necessary to cast these buildings in the desired light. This filter is, of course, simply the instrumental dimension of what we have described as the Tugendhat paradigm, applied retroactively in Krefeld as a historical corrective. The removal of select wall fragments, the periodic sprinkling with Mies furniture (a metonymy, of course, for the architect himself), the lack of interest in period images and items, and the celebration through exquisitely crafted images of architectural conditions made possible only by altering the built work: these actions are intended to help us recover the presence of Mies from the miasma of historically contingent circumstances that dogged the Krefeld villas.

The only obstacle to this project is that the historically contingent circumstances are arguably not contingent, but originary. This is an architecture originally designed to coexist with, rather than co-opt, the life it sheltered. It is incomplete, in the sense of having limited—not compromised—its scope. It is also overly complete, in the sense of possessing subtly disfiguring accommodations like the small organ chamber and various partition walls. Positing the Krefeld villas as commensurate with the dominant Mies paradigm therefore required both erasure (to remove the disfigurations) and additions (to legitimize Mies's creative presence). The goal of this effort was to position the villas comfortably as transitional works, stronger in conception than in execution. This was the project undertaken by Storck and his successors, and it has been executed with admirable sophistication, care, and success.

There is another way to approach the Krefeld works, one that requires fewer modifications of the historic record. The alternative is to posit the villas as precise responses by a fully modern architect to a given set of pre-existing conditions. The virtue of this approach is to explore a mode of modern architecture that had to invent an aesthetic response that was both critical and accommodating, an architecture that would bring together in one material and spatial formulation incommensurate forces. Seen in this light, the central questions raised by the Krefeld villas are these: Can an architecture hover so close to a value system it purports to undermine? Is such an architecture still modern? A conventional bourgeois milieu within a modern shell residing comfortably together, even contaminating one another, runs counter to modernity's image and certainly to that of Mies van der Rohe's architecture. What is the nature of this coexistence? Is the relationship between the work of this architect and the culture it housed more complex than the usual trope of "reflectivity"? What if Mies's work never actually reflected or expressed the modern epoch it purportedly reflected and expressed, but rather compensated for its deficiencies, expressed that which it was not, and provided for that which was missing? In short, what if Mies's work was a form of compensation?

The notion that a modernist practice—in art and in architecture—could have a compensatory relationship with bourgeois culture rather than a revolutionary one is not typically the way modernist practices have been described. Yet there is a large body of thought, associated with writers such as Max Horkheimer, Theodor Adorno, Herbert Marcuse, and, more recently, Peter Bürger, that sees modernism as a buttress for, rather than a battering ram against, the very conditions the modern movement ostensibly sought to undermine. Bürger describes the compensatory relationship between art and society as follows:

> All those needs that cannot be satisfied in everyday life, because the principle of competition pervades all spheres, can find a home in art, because art is removed from the praxis of life. Values such as humanity, joy, truth, solidarity are extruded from life as it were, and preserved in art. In bourgeois society, art has a contradictory role: it projects the image of a better order and to that extent protests against the bad order that prevails. But by realizing the existence of a better order in fiction,... it relieves the existing society of the pressure of those forces that make for change. They are assigned to confinement in an ideal sphere.[25]

The only effective alternative to the contradictory role of art was to be found in the work of the historical avant-garde, who consciously and strategically sought to close the distance between art and the praxis of life so that art could potentially change, rather than merely affirm, life. In this sense, modernism and the avant-garde are two distinct practices with very different socio-cultural agendas.

If tinkering with the praxis of life was the principal pleasure and labor of the avant-garde, one cannot easily include Mies in that camp, for Mies was famously disdainful and distant from precisely these pleasures and labors. But Mies's work does seem consistent with the affirmative or compensatory function of modernism described by Bürger. Indeed, "realizing the existence of a better order in fiction"

overleaf
[23]   Klein with fire-wall, Museum Haus Lange,
1961

could serve as a rubric for any number of Mies's accomplishments, from the hand-laid bricks with their machine-like precision to the machine-like chair that no industrial process could yield. Over the course of Mies's career, his work becomes progressively less involved in any actual way with the forces and methods of the industrial epoch, and by the time Mies had established his reputation in the United States, the gap between his practice and the organization of productive relations—the praxis of life—was vast. As Mies's late work became obsessively dedicated to the proposition of perfectibility, America's mass-market economy was fully in the grip of planned obsolescence. Mies had become the essential antidote to, rather than the expression of, the thrust of the dominant material culture. Bürger would undoubtedly see the rational, perfectible Miesian tower as a clear example of the affirmative project.

All this is nascent in the Krefeld work. What Lange and Esters sought, and what Mies appears to have given, was a confirmation that certain traditional values were compatible with rapid modernization. Consider the image of Lange's Biedermeier desk against the backdrop of what was then one of the largest sheets of glazing in a residential setting. The Krefeld villas can be seen as a palliative for contemporary society, as a means of coping with society's unrealized promises, and as more and not less compatible with—indeed necessary for—a bourgeois ethos lodged in an industrialized era.

LeWitt and the Art of Instructions [1]

In October 1969, Sol LeWitt installed seven gridded sculptures in, and drew on the walls of, Haus Lange. In the large hall on the ground floor, four basic drawing components were introduced in four separate drawings, each in the same 190-centimeters square format: vertical lines, horizontal lines, diagonal lines from lower left to upper right, and diagonal lines from upper left to lower right, white walls furrowed with lines of hard lead.[1] All possible combinations of the four basic elements were played out in the eleven remaining drawings dispersed throughout the villa. For the exhibition catalogue, the wall drawings were redrawn: fifteen drawings, ink on paper, reproduced at about 3 inches square.

While the LeWitt exhibition occurred near the beginning of the artist's prolific career, the nascent practice already contained features of his mature work. LeWitt would author over 700 wall drawings in the next decade alone, but almost none would be drawn by the artist himself. Instead, LeWitt authors instruction sets: explicit directions for an array of assistants, school children, museum staff, artists, and gallery friends who execute the drawings on museum and gallery walls throughout the world. The instructions range from the minimal (*Lines in Four Directions, Each in a Quarter of a Square*, 1969) to the exhaustive (such as the 45 lines of text yielding a single line in the 1975 *The Location of a Line* series).[2] Beginning in 1984, LeWitt augmented the instruction sets with additional specifications for materials and techniques to be used in producing a wall drawing: the primer ("Aqualock, two coats"), the paint ("Regal Satin Latex, Decorator white #215-01 [Benjamin Moore]"), the pencils ("Koh-I-Noor 22000 Series—2 mm leads"), the graphite ("8H or 9H"), and

[1]   Sol LeWitt, *Three Cubes*, Museum Haus Lange, 1969

[1]

the technique ("in drawings where there are multiple lines approximately 1/8" apart, five sharpened pencil leads are bundled together, so that the second and the fourth leads are spacers and the draftsman is able to draw three lines at one time").[3] More and more, it became possible for anyone with a modicum of manual dexterity and substantial patience to execute a LeWitt.

Almost predictably, the instructions themselves took on the deferred aura of the artwork.[4] The instructions for a drawing were typically affixed to the wall, adjacent to the drawings themselves; LeWitt explained that having both the instructions and the consequences of the instructions in close proximity was programmatically significant:

> If I do a wall drawing, I have to have the plan written on the wall or label
> because it aids the understanding of the idea. If I just had lines on the wall,
> no one would know that there are ten thousand lines within a certain space,
> so I have two kinds of form—the lines, and the explanation of the lines.[5]

Of course the instructions are more the refusal of an explanation, as Rosalind Krauss points out in an essay on the artist, more like "a guide's telling his listener how high this particular redwood is,"[6] articulating the "how" but emphatically not the "what" or "why." In architectural parlance, this type of instrumental text is familiar from specifications—those prescriptive, procedural instructions that describe the scope and quality of the construction work to be done. Missing is only the binding "shall be" language that turns a description into a directive for construction, as in: "[there shall be] Ten Thousand Lines, 5" Long, Within a 7" Square."[7]

The production of specifications and instructions rather than crafted artifacts was a central tactic of a generation of artists alternately called "minimalists," "conceptualists," or "literalists." Foregrounding a work's procedural machinery, focusing on process and formal operations, was a critical and self-conscious device for terminating an artwork's relationship to both illusionism and to the internal life of the artist. At stake was the production of a new site for signification. Without recourse to traditional sources of meaning—the emotional state of the artist, the nature of the subject matter, myth, narrative, genre—the artwork was set adrift in the public realm without parentage, without a cord back to anything other than the facts of its material condition. To the degree that meaning could be forged, it would do so through bodily engagement, in the present, comparable, according to one scholar, to the mode in which language finds its content.[8]

Instructions deflected questions of signification away from the work's originating moment and into a kind of distended present, since there was clearly nothing to be gained by traveling backward in time to, say, early sketches or experiences. Traveling forward, however, required a degree of interaction between artwork and beholder—physically and psychically—that was inherently temporal. It is this extended temporality, and the explicit incorporation of the observer with the artwork, that prompted art historian Michael Fried to observe that what he termed "literalist art" had crossed genre boundaries from the visual arts to the performing arts to theater.[9] Fried offered this observation critically, understanding theater as the essential enemy of the visual arts. Minimalist art did indeed do violence to the idea that art should be *present* (rather than, as in minimalist pieces, temporally extended); the beholder should be *denied* (rather than addressed, in the sense of an audience); and the artwork should be *absorbed* (rather than acknowledging the presence of a beholder). These were all characteristics that Fried determined were essential for what he termed the "great fiction" of painting as articulated already in eighteenth-century French art criticism.[10] This violence was not just the outcome of the works the minimalists made, but also of the way these works came into the world. The assault on conventional art was in a sense authenticated, documented, and certified by the step-by-step instructions that governed the forming of many minimalist projects. Thus LeWitt, always one of the more consequent of his contemporaries, insisted that his instructions be posted right next to his wall drawings, for the work, or at least the way the work was made, would otherwise be inexplicable.

When LeWitt drew on Mies's Haus Lange, many detected an almost natural affinity. There were predicable (though hardly sustainable) claims that Mies and LeWitt shared a common formal vocabulary. Even museum director Paul Wember gravitated toward the idea of a formal heritage as the common root between artist and architect, declaring in the opening paragraph of the exhibition catalogue,

> In the beginning there was the cube; that is commensurate for Sol LeWitt as well as for Ludwig Mies van der Rohe. Many artists have arranged their work inspired through this house. The work of some artists fits especially well

within this frame. Never before were Architecture and Sculpture in such correlation. There seems to be a mental identity between the sculptures of Sol LeWitt and the architectural volume of Ludwig Mies van der Rohe.[11]

Despite such questionable formal analogies—since the cube as either a volume or a module appears nowhere in the architect's oeuvre—the similarity between Mies and LeWitt can be read on two levels. The first level is quite obvious: LeWitt was explicit about his cross-disciplinary raid on architectural techniques of product delivery. Referring to his brief stint working for the architect I. M. Pei, LeWitt observed that "working in an architectural office, meeting architects, knowing architects had a big effect. An architect doesn't go off with a shovel and dig his foundation and lay every brick."[12] LeWitt's work shares with architecture its techniques of projection (plans, elevations and axonometric drawings), its materials (cinderblock, aluminum tubing, house paint), and the mode—and problems—of authenticating a work. Plans and specifications, the so-called "instruments of service," constitute the legally defined and protected work of an architect; LeWitt's practice of authenticating his wall drawings by issuing autographed diagrams and instruction certificates parallels this model.

The second similarity is more subtle, and yet more essential—namely, the tactical deployment of instructions not merely as a means of mobilizing hired hands, but as a means for effectively barricading a work against signification. The equivalent to LeWitt's "Ten Thousand Lines" peppers Mies's recorded utterances: "It is our specific concern to liberate building activity from aesthetic speculators and make building again what alone it should be, namely BUILDING."[13] Again and again, in Mies's own words and in the words of his commentators, we are reminded of the importance of *bauen* (building), of Mies as *Baukünstler* (building artist) rather than architect, of Mies's designs as the result of reasoned assemblage, of the meaningfulness "when two bricks are brought together in a significant way."[14] Particularly in the early texts written in the 1920s, Mies deploys descriptions of assembly as a defense around his work, emphatically and tautologically discouraging any meandering readings. *Bauen* formed the ground for architecture: one could rise from there into spiritual matters, into the realm of *Baukunst*, but one could not, as it were, get behind or around *bauen* into its metaphoric/expressive/symbolic sources, just as one could not get behind LeWitt's instructions. What should building be? "Building," Mies tells us. What are those horizontal lines? "Horizontal lines," the label next to the drawing tells us.

It is almost irresistible not to say more about *bauen* or lines. LeWitt was remarkably coy, offering only sporadic suggestions that there is an "idea" driving his vast enterprise: "neither lines nor words are ideas, they are the means by which ideas are conveyed."[15] LeWitt's relative silence on this matter has been hugely profitable in the sense that the field is left open for the speculations of any number of commentators. Mies was slightly less reserved—and left less to the imagination—in his statements about the relationship between what he saw as the raw facts of *bauen* and higher-level aspirations—aspirations having to do with expressions of the epoch. He was quite clear about the priority of concerns that would lead to such expressions, with the conditions of *bauen* being first and foremost, as if a recognizable Zeitgeist would necessarily spring from rigorous tectonics, but rigorous tectonics would not necessarily spring from a preoccupation with grandiose ideas. Mies's educational roadmap was to guide his students "over the road of discipline from materials, through function, to creative work."[16] The degree to which Mies trusted in the disciplining value of rigorous assembly is revealed in a statement recorded by his colleague, Reginald Malcolmson, who was to become one of the most stalwart defenders of the Miesian ethic: "If I had to build a free-standing wall in brick, plastered on all sides, so that the bricks themselves could not be seen, I would still build the brick wall in English bond."[17]

How would you know that there are ten thousand lines? How would you know it is English bond? Persuading the mind of that which the eye cannot see is part and parcel of establishing the authority of process. Any number of late-twentieth-century artworks exist on two planes: as a set of effects and as stories of their becoming. LeWitt is somewhat typical of his generation, if not his discipline, in this regard. But architecture is less direct, more mediated—in a sense, more fictional—than art. Even an architect such as Antonio Gaudi—who, with his use of funicular models, appears to have relinquished his form-making to the automatism of gravity—surrendered only a small part of architecture to an apparently objective process. Recently the work of Gaudi has been contrasted with that of Mies, using the former to demonstrate a more rational approach than the latter, and thus exposing our visual bias for equating Mies's simplicity and orthogonality, as opposed to Gaudi's complexity and curvaceousness, with rational procedures.[18] But even Gaudi fails to satisfy the dictates of a predominantly objective architecture: gravity in no way determines the length of Gaudi's tensile members, the resolution of thrust or, most obviously, the entire composition of the plan. Given the difficulty of identifying any historically based practice that claims a rational basis, Mies's faith in the profound discipline of construction was strikingly strident and resolute. It is precisely because it was so strident and resolute that it seemed exaggerated, improbable, and fragile.

This fragility accounts for one of the more curious aspects in Miesian scholarship—namely the invention of instruction diagrams for projects long *after* their conception, inverting the purported causal relationship between construction imperatives and building form. A case in point is the often reproduced set of brick coursing details and the finely articulated ground plan for the Brick Country House, drawn under Mies's supervision by Werner Blaser in 1965 and published over four decades after the house was conceived. [2, 3] The information contained in these extraordinary drawings, in which every brick is depicted, have virtually no basis in the original delineations. It should be recalled that the original drawings for the Brick Country House consisted of only two images: a plan rendered in light pencil outline with the wall *poché* filled in with charcoal, and a perspective view that differs slightly in proportions and composition from the plan.[19] In his 1965 book, *Mies van der Rohe: The Art of Structure*, in which the drawings first appeared, Blaser states, "the ground plan of the brick house is a good example of the manner in which Mies van der Rohe developed the art of the structure from the very beginning. The structure of a brick wall begins already with the smallest divisible unit: the brick."[20] This claim that the design was informed by the rigorous dictates of the humble brick, right down to the wall thicknesses and the dimensions of the fenestration is, of course, blatantly untrue. It is true, however, that by 1965 it was deemed important to both Mies and Blaser to issue what amounts to a *post-facto* manifesto on Mies's method, as if to secure both project and method from alternative wayward readings, such as the persistent (and from Mies's perspective, inaccurate) comparison of the original Brick Country House plan to De Stijl paintings, particularly Theo van Doesburg's 1918 *Rhythm of a Russian Dance*.[21] If the building had been executed, the manifesto proclaims, the instructions

[2]   Mies's Brick Country House Project (1924), detail of plan drawn by Werner Blaser in 1965

[3]   Brick Country House Project, axonometric, drawn by Werner Blaser in 1965

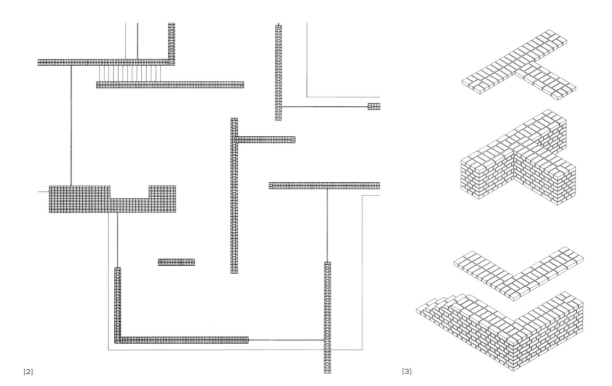

[2]

[3]

would have specified perfect English bonding and rigorous modularity, right through to the core of the massive chimney blocks. Presumably then, this also applies to those buildings that were executed, in brick, in English bond, in the late 1920s: Haus Lange and Haus Esters.

Almost without exception, to the degree that Haus Lange and Haus Esters are cited at all, it is through the lens of their construction, and understandably so. Both villas are bearing-wall construction, both are executed in English bond, and—almost a direct test of Mies's tectonic commitment—both are plastered on the inside with exposed brick on the outside. There is an abundance of drawings related to the brick-work of both villas that support a reading that privileges the role played by the "humble brick." At the large scale of 1:20, Mies had all the elevations of the villas drawn with enough individual bricks depicted (although not the apocryphal *every* brick) to determine the exact layout of each brick on each surface. [4] On a typical drawing, a vertical scale was included in the left-hand margin, divided into units of brick coursing. To the right of the scale, a schematic wall section showed the significant vertical measurements—floors, window and door sills, and heads—in terms of multiples of this dimension, as well as in absolute metric measure. The elevations specified an English bond, alternating courses of headers (the short face of the brick) and stretchers (the long face), with stretcher courses becoming header courses and visa-versa as the pattern turns a corner. The pattern was uninflected by architectural, even structural, contingencies: window heads on the north and south elevations are all header courses, whereas east- and west-facing window heads are correspondingly stretcher courses. Significant horizontal dimensions were indicated on the elevations in multiples of the smallest unit, the dimension of the head of a brick. On the elevations, headers are designated with the letter "K" (for *Klinker*) and mortar joints are designated with the letter "F" (for *Fuge.)* Each dimension line is accompanied by a simple formula of "K" and "F" variables as well as an overall dimension in metric units (for example, 5K+4F=56.5 cm).

The entire brick layout, however, cannot be resolved with just headers and full stretchers. Since the bond pattern requires successive courses to be staggered, a 3/4 brick length is required at the corners and endings of each stretcher course. [5] Thus there are two basic brick types, reducible to a single unit module that is the dimension of the head of a brick. It is obvious that the system was designed to effectively

[4]   Haus Lange, working drawing of south elevation, 1928

[5]   3/4 brick at edge condition

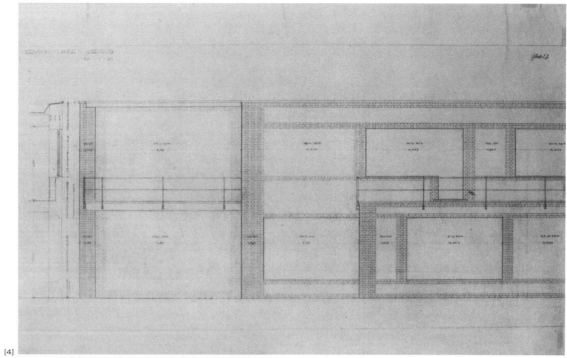

[4]

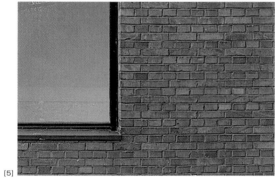

[5]

minimize the number of fundamental modules involved in assembling these facades. There are no fractions of modules, and openings and wall lengths are multiples of a few basic measurements. Solving the simple equations reveals the following values for the two brick types:

Type 1: 5 cm high, 10.5 cm head face, 22 cm stretcher face
Type 2: 5 cm high, 10.5 cm head face, 16.25 cm stretcher face
Joints: 1 cm

It is important to recall that these units, and the pattern for their assembly, are derived from the elevation drawings only. There are no drawings indicating the corresponding arrangement in plan, nor are there sections in which the wall thickness is articulated in terms of brick units. What we can derive from the documentary record are instructions for producing a resolved surface condition, more accurately termed the *coursing* for the walls (i.e. a two-dimensional surface pattern), rather than *bonding* (i.e. a three-dimensional structural matrix). Yet it is entirely likely that these elevations informed Blaser's bonding diagrams for the unbuilt Brick Country House, which are based on the same English bond brick pattern as the Krefeld villas and not on the Flemish bond surface of Mies's other contemporaneous and substantial brick residence, Haus Wolf. If the Krefeld villas inspired Blaser's drawings, the drawings soon reciprocated. Blaser's interpolation inspired Mies commentators to read the surface information contained in the Krefeld elevations as an index of a tectonically pure assembly, and to subscribe to the notion of a homogeneous wall of stacked bricks of a single, originating type as depicted in the diagrams. Kenneth Frampton, for example, published the Brick Country House bonding diagrams adjacent to an elevation fragment of Haus Lange on the same page as his narrative on the Krefeld villa, captioning the Blaser image with "*Typical* brick coursing by Mies (reconstruction by Werner Blaser for the Brick Country House of 1923)."[22]

Faith is necessary if one is to see, in the precise instructions contained on the elevation drawings of the Krefeld villas, or on the brick surfaces themselves, the mark of a thorough tectonic discipline. It is necessary because the bonding patterns in the drawings for Haus Esters and Haus Lange are not, in fact, three-dimensional instructions. They do not implicate building in its profound sense, as voiced by

Mies—as an activity with spatial consequences, or even one that produces an outcome transparent to the process of its making. It is no coincidence that LeWitt, in compiling instructions for a fully three-dimensional work such as the *Cinderblock Piece*, did several drawings, plans and elevations, for elevations on their own are insufficient instructions.[23] [6] The Krefeld elevations are rather more like LeWitt's wall drawings: rigorously constructed surfaces made up of essentially two-dimensional modules; surfaces that wrap around corners but are not inherently "thick." In short, the brickwork of Haus Lange and Haus Esters is a veneer, in the most literal sense.

The instructions for laying up the exposed brick walls are contained in the contract documents for Haus Lange prepared for the masonry contractors. The specifications for the exposed brickwork are as follows:

> The facing of the perimeter walls as a supplement to the masonry of the basement level, with Bockhorner clinkers (size 22/10, 5/5, 2) of premier grade, colored, omitting the completely blue and the yellowish bricks, 3 courses, beginning below ground in block bond as per drawings and specifications, 16 facing courses up to 1 meter with triple tieback, joints pointed 1 cm deep and brushed clean, including delivery of all materials. Pay particular attention to insure that the glazing corners face downwards.[24]

The specifications for the basement-level brickwork, referenced in the first sentence above, read in part as follows:

> cbm [cubic meters] masonry for the 63 cm thick walls of the basement level of first class ring-oven bricks with lime-mortar 1:6, in good cross bonding. [25]

The expensive, partially vitrified clinkers from the Dutch firm Bockhorner, with their purple-red finish, were used to face a masonry wall made up of more ordinary bricks. The interior of the walls, the structural core, was laid up in a cross bond, for which there were no drawings—standard masonry construction apparently being assumed on the part of the architect. Wall thicknesses are described by the contractor elsewhere as being either 12, 25, 38, 51, or 64 centimeters, except in the case of the exposed clinker walls, which were dimensioned on the plans.[26] A wall thickness of 50 centimeters is typical for the perimeter walls of both villas. The clinkers were to be laid up in a block bond, which is essentially a simple vertical stacking of the stones, a single wythe, with only every fourth course tied back to the structural wall with a stretcher brick for stability. Thus, every other header course is in fact not a full stone but a half-clinker, or a third brick type born only of efficiency and economy.

The bricks in the interior of the wall measure approximately 23 x 12 x 5.5 centimeters and bear no modular relation to the size of the clinkers. [7] A 2-centimeter-wide tolerance gap exists between the structural core and the facing clinkers to absorb the dimensional slack between the rough interior bricks and the precisely specified finish dimension of the clinkers. [8] On a number of section drawings for the villas, the indeterminate relationship between the clinker-facing bricks and the load-bearing bricks proper is surprisingly explicit: the clinkers are drawn stone by stone, while the remaining wall is depicted with hatched linework. [9] On the interior, the rough bricks are hidden behind several coats of white plaster. In short, their extraordinary exterior is the product of a conventional wall section.

Mies's brick villas are apparently in need of the same type of explanation—or defense—that has by now become a standard addendum to any discussion of his work in steel, or his so-called "industrial" furniture, or his rationality, or the general issue regarding truth in architecture. Perhaps this is not surprising; indeed, it might even be seen as a desirable consistency on the part of the architect. But bricks, and the lore of brickwork, have been privileged in the shaping of Mies's reputation. Bricks play a foundational role in the biographical tales told of Mies's humble experiences in the building trades during his apprenticeship years in Aachen prior his makeover into a Berliner cosmopolite. Mies's use of exposed brick in the 1920s in five works—the Brick Country House Project of 1924, Haus Wolf of 1925–27, the Liebknecht-Luxemburg Monument of 1926, and Haus Lange and Haus Esters of 1927–30—has been understood as his tribute and connection to a timeless craft of building, that which made him (in a positive sense) unmodern or "transmodern." According to Philip Johnson, Mies appreciated the fact that brick was one of the few structural materials that rendered its own finished surface, that did not need to be concealed, and that tested to the full the consequences of technique on expression. It was also Johnson who first reported the extraordinary measures Mies would go to when

[6]   LeWitt, *Cinderblock Piece*, plan and
       elevation, 1991

[7]   Typical glazed Clinker (top) and rough interior
       Ziegelstein (bottom)

[8]   Rough interior bricks exposed during 2000
       restoration of the villas

[9]   Wall section indicating brick veneer

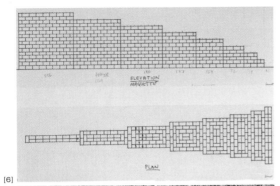

[6]

[7]

[8]

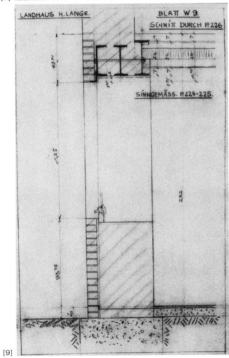

[9]

building in brick, claiming that "in order to insure the evenness of the bonding at corners and apertures, he calculated all dimensions in brick lengths and occasionally went so far as to separate the under-fired long bricks from the over-fired short ones, using the long in one dimension and the short in the other."[27] Mies has consequently been credited with coaxing a machined precision out of the handiwork of bricklaying to the point where the masonry units and mortar joints merged to form an overall texture of such regularity that it approached the appearance of an industrialized surface. Craft was pushed to a degree of such perfection that it disappeared.[28]

Much of this lore is easily dismissed as just that: tales that seem more necessary than necessarily true. The "separation of bricks" episode cannot be verified on the basis of the Krefeld buildings, wherein any given course of bricks vary as one might expect in a brick wall.[29] Mies may not, in fact, have had much of a role in controlling the quality of the bricks or their laying up. In a letter to the architect during the first weeks of construction dated November 12, 1928, Josef Esters insisted that Mies make time during a scheduled trip to Krefeld to review the already completed Bockhorner cladding of the exposed east-facing basement wall of his villa, presumably the first wall to be bricked up: "We think it necessary for you to take a look at the effect [of the clinkers], particularly since Herr Walther had to reject the first load of bricks because of their uneven size and the pronounced differences in color among them."[30] The impression is that the brickwork was progressing on a schedule independent of the architect's direct supervision and involvement.

Perhaps even more to the point, however, Mies's reputed obsession does not make particular sense in terms of masonry construction with nonindustrial raw units. Given both an absolute overall dimension and a coursing pattern, it is the play of the law of averages that permits both requirements to be fulfilled by the mason. If only shorter bricks are sorted and used, the overall dimension can only be achieved with oversized joints; using only longer bricks, the opposite problem occurs. The 22-centimeter stretcher dimension used by Mies in producing the elevation drawings is a virtual dimension only, and only a mixed batch of imperfect units can produce it. In other words, too much precision would paradoxically result in gross misalignment. The same argument, of course, applies to the joints. In the absence of an industrialized raw unit material, handicraft is required to yield an industrialized appearance. This was not lost on Mies; in fact, he apparently appreciated the subtle variations

[10] Haus Esters, precise brickwork executed around edges of windows

[11] Haus Esters, west facade, anomalies in brick coursing

[10]

[11]

that attend to brick surfaces: "How sensible is this small handy shape, so useful for every purpose," he said in 1938. "What logic in its bonding, what liveliness in the play of patterns. What richness in the simplest wall surface."[31]

This richness is the sum of precision and chance—the great invention of the surrealists, who recognized that the aleatory is only legible within a framework of regulations. It emerges, in Mies, by presenting the natural grain of a given material —be it veined onyx, marbled ebony, reflective chromium, or variegated glazing— within a frame of overt geometrical control. Mies exercised this control most stringently at the edges of his surfaces; his preferred tool was the razor blade. His marble, his wood, his brick veneers are all terminated by the same gesture: a cut. The greatest precision in the brickwork of Haus Lange and Haus Esters is to be found at the edges—around the windows, at the corners, at the bottoms and tops of wall surfaces. [10] This is also why the anomalies in the reportedly "perfect English bond"—and there are some to be found despite the careful calculations and strident proclamations—never occur at the extremities of a brick plane but are always slipped away into the interior of the surface to become part of its richness. [11]

"All wall drawings contain errors, they are part of the work."[32] A degree of elasticity is to be anticipated, appreciated, and is in any case an inevitable part of the relationship between instructions and execution. At issue, however, is not the elasticity of the relationship, but its productivity. Is a cause-effect mechanism in fact necessary to produce the desired cause-effect *effect*, or can the effect, as it were, be simulated with sufficiently careful artifice? LeWitt, at least, was not adverse to artifice. When asked, "Does the number 10,000 stand for a very large number or infinity? When you use it, what does it indicate?" he responded, "Many."[33]

So let us not count or quibble about accurate accounting, because to do so already betrays a lack of conviction, a failure. The point is to inquire into the conditions, factual and fictitious, that allow a work to be understood as the product of an operation and a discipline relatively internal to the material at hand and relatively immune to the idiosyncratic impulses of the authoring agent or stylizing culture. Veracity seems not to be the condition, although perhaps the claim thereto is. Words matter. "Brick-clad Country Villa" or even "Country Villa in Neubabelsberg" would, after all, be a far more accurate title for the canonized "Brick Country House."

overleaf

[12] Haus Esters, service and main entrances

But this would divert our attention to a host of questions about contingencies—program, budget, site constraints, orientation, context, the nature of the missing second-floor plan, to name only the most obvious—that a siteless, material exercise effectively dodges.[34]

If the integrity of operationally based practices—in LeWitt, in Mies, and in general—appears to be slipping (from 10,000 lines to many lines, from English bond to an English bond pattern), it is not slipping *downward* from truth to falsehood, but sliding *laterally*—if not actually *upward*—from truth in fact to truth in fiction. Artifice is an indispensable tool in producing works that desire both a procedural provenance and a formal outcome. In Mies's Krefeld houses an extraordinary degree of artifice is deployed to construct the fiction that these structures are but the imperatives of masonry traditions re-processed and re-presented through a modern sensibility. This architecture is not materially and tectonically determined; the bonding is not rigorous; the module is not pervasive and cannot regulate the whole; and refined brickwork is not hidden behind the plastered interior surfaces. But the greatest fiction, great in the sense of most compellingly presented, has not yet been discussed—namely, the reception of these two buildings as "the brick villas." For in fact, but not in fiction, they might just as accurately be called "the steel villas."

Serra and the Anti-Environment

November 28, 1983

Dear Clara Weyergraf, dear Richard Serra,

Includes [sic] you find the floors plans of Haus Lange and Haus Esters. I tried to find out the maximum weight to be put on the floor—but nobody knows exact dates [sic]. (There are only experienced dates [sic] *(Erfahrungs-werte)* gathered in different exhibitions. The floor is good for high weight if the weight is not concentrated on one point but spread. A steel plate of the length like in Bochum, not quite as high will not create any problems, prob-ably. To support the floor from underneath with props is not really useful since we don't know the exact placing of the steel carriers *(Stahlträger.)*...I hope this will be of help. Looking forward to see [sic] you in spring,

best wishes,

(Marianne Stockebrand)[1]

On January 20, 1985, an exhibition of Richard Serra's sculptures and drawings opened in Museum Haus Lange. Serra conceived of all but one of the eleven pieces expressly for the villa: four original works in steel located on the ground floor and six charcoal drawings for the bedrooms on the upper level.[2] The largest sculptural piece, installed in the living room, consisted of two steel plates bisecting diago-nally opposite corners of the room, each projecting nearly eight meters into the room, supported only by virtue of their positioning in the corners and by the inertia of their own substantial weight. Serra entitled the piece *Two 45° Angles for Mies.* [1, 2]

[1]   Richard Serra, *Two 45° Angles for Mies*, Museum
      Haus Lange, 1985

[1]

[2]

[2]   *Two 45° Angles for Mies*
[3]   Serra, *Klein's Walls*, Museum Haus Lange, 1985

[3]

From the living room, one caught sight of the second piece, installed along a wall in the former man's room, partially blocking its entrance. There were two sheets again: one flush along the wall surface, the second tipped precariously against the first. The title of the piece, *Klein's Wall*, recalls the history of the small chamber directly behind, and supporting, the plates. [3] The third work, *Mies' Corner Extended*, consisted of two steel plates of unequal lengths positioned in a corner of the former drawing room, one element extending beyond the corner into space, the other propped at right angles to stabilize the first. [4] The last new work on the ground level, *Unequal Corner Elevations*, was installed in the former woman's room. Two small but dense blocks of forged steel were positioned in opposing corners along the west wall. Their dimensions were 43 x 43 x 45 centimeters and 44 x 44 x 46.5 centimeters, respectively—just shy of cubic, just shy of equal. [5] In each case, the titles referred to the site for which the work was conceived.

By 1985, the year of the exhibition, Serra's attitude regarding the relationship between his sculptural work and its architectural setting had become the source of much critical attention and scrutiny. In a contemporaneous publication issued by *Galerie m*, whose owner, Alexander von Berswordt-Wallrabe, played a central role in the Krefeld show, Serra outlined this relationship:

> I think that sculpture, if it has any potential at all, has the potential to cre-
> ate its own place and space, and to work in contradiction to the places and
> spaces where it is created. I am interested in work where the artist is a
> maker of "anti-environment" which takes its own place or makes its own
> situation.... In my work I analyze the site and determine to redefine it in
> terms of sculpture.... I'm not interested in affirmation.[3]

The concept of the anti-environment is central to understanding Serra's site-specific sculptural oeuvre and specifically the installation in Haus Lange. Certainly one aspiration of the anti-environment project is that it would serve as a type of ideological litmus test, one that would precipitate and reveal a dominant hierarchy in a given environment by positing a counterreading of the site. This stance would frequently put Serra at odds with both those commissioning work and, equally frequently it seems, with architects, whom Serra sees as natural allies to the power structure inherent in

[4]   Serra, *Mies' Corner Extended*, Museum Haus
       Lange, 1985

[5]   Serra, *Unequal Corner Elevations*, Museum Haus
       Lange, 1985

[4]

[5]

the very nature of architectural commissions. Serra cites repeatedly the episode involving his initial involvement with—and subsequent withdrawal from—the Venturi/Scott Brown proposal for the Pennsylvania Avenue Development Commission, in which the architects' framing of the United States Treasury Building with two flag-topped pylons was opposed by Serra for its overt ideological pandering. Serra's counterproposal—one block perpendicular to an inclined plaza—was rejected.[4] The conflict, of course, was not new; any number of artists produce work critical of the very socio-political class structure that yields patrons, collectors, and edifying architectural settings.

Notwithstanding attempts to see Serra's raw industrial materials and non-affirming stance as a materialist critique of capitalism and its institutions, the artist's anti-environments were not only—and probably not even primarily—politically motivated.[5] In the end, it is reductive to hold Serra's anti-environments accountable to any particular advocacy position; we hardly need an inclined plaza to remind us of the societal weight of the U.S. Treasury. Rather, his installations attempt to reveal the workings of a situation's spatial matrix by placing within that matrix a sculptural, rather than a political, counterweight. In speaking of his 1992 installation *Weight and Measure* at the Duveen Galleries at the Tate Gallery in London, Serra described his intentions:

> The architecture [of the Duveen Galleries] as a whole is overblown, authoritarian and a bit heavy-handed. It is a little bit "Thou shalt walk this way and then take the side aisles." What I wanted to do, and what I hope I am doing, is to bring another relevance to that space. I do not want to reinforce the intentionality of the architecture but redirect how one thinks about it. I want to expose it.[6]

This "it" is not authoritarianism per se, but the architectural scaffold that causes the space to feel authoritarian. What Serra does, or does best, is not dismantle the hierarchy-producing machinery of institutions, but the space-making machinery of architecture. At the Tate, for example, Serra addressed not the institutions that made the work possible—to list the corporate sponsors would quickly render this proposition a farce—but rather the architectural circumstances that formed the work's counterpart. Serra felt the position of the gallery's octagonal hall was a "big trap":

It reads as a separate vertical volume and, without being an actual pedestal, it takes on the function of a pedestal.... I needed to come up with a solution which avoided this overly defined focal point.[7]

The columns were also problematic:

[T]hey have an enormous sculptural presence. Once you acknowledge the columns you acknowledge the vertical scale of the room.[8]

Finally, Serra wished to draw out the predictability of the gallery's symmetry:

The width as well as the height of the elements [two unequal rectangular blocks] were crucial decisions. When you enter the Tate Gallery both blocks will appear equal. I don't think that you will realise their difference in elevation until you enter the central octagon and look back and forth.... one element reads as a horizontal volume, its top plane clearly below eye level, whereas the other will rise vertically above your eye level as you walk towards it. It reverses the expectation.[9]

A great deal of architectural analysis by Serra preceded any sculptural conception. He had to do significantly more than sculpt two rectangular blocks of forged steel, for he could not figure an anti-environment without first having produced a reading of the architectural setting: the anti-environment's environment.

When Serra installed work in Mies's Haus Lange, a productive interaction between artist and architecture was all but preprogrammed and highly anticipated. Serra was no stranger to Mies's work. In fact, he held Mies in unusually high regard as one of the great constructors of the modern era, together with the likes of John Roebling, Gustav Eiffel, Robert Maillart, and Antonio Gaudi.[10] And while Serra's exhibition was to be an exploration of the spatiality of Mies's brick villa and not a direct interrogation of its tectonics, the two aspects were, as always and everywhere with Mies, held to be causally linked. In fact, this perceived linkage was the source of Serra's respect for the architect. Pairing the nature of Serra's sculptural interventions with the architectural character of Haus Lange dominated the critical interpretation of the exhibition. Marianne Stockebrand's observation in her exhibition catalogue essay was typical:

> In Haus Lange one is repeatedly impressed by the generosity and transparency of the open and interlocking spaces.... The giant steel plates on the ground floor of Haus Lange are positioned such that the expansiveness of the spaces is hemmed in, the spatial flow is interrupted, and the vistas are disrupted.[11]

In particular, Serra's *Two 45° Angles for Mies* was understood as a direct opposition to the lexicon of the villa's orthogonal geometry.[12] More than that, however, it was understood as a counterweight to the villa's dominant spatiality. The steel plates disrupted the ability to sense the geometry of the space by introducing an acute angle, producing a parallelogram of space—an unstable, dynamic figure foreign to the obstinate orthogonal order of the villa's footprint. The two 45° plates, placed in opposite corners of the rectangular living room, produced a discontinuous diagonal. Plate and edge adopted shifting relations as the viewer moved through the room.

The remaining three interior interventions were also understood as precise countermoves stimulated by the architectural setting. *Klein's Wall* and *Mies' Corner Extended*, for example, both narrowed the plan's spatial flow, pinching it with steel plates that operated like half-closed sliding doors. Both pieces involved one unstable plate being supported by a second unstable plate, one reaching out precipitously in plan, the other tipped precariously in section. Serra's walls were thus the antithesis of the sturdy, load-bearing supports of Haus Lange. This is a repeated theme: the structurally rational, compositionally determined, and perceptually stable presence of the brick villa was made more palpable by the structurally daring, compositionally contingent, and perceptually osculating presence of Serra's anti-environment. "*Anlehnen und querstellen*"–"leaning on and crossing out"–was the phrase of choice;[13] one commentator, praising the exhibition, described the overall installation as "a comprehensive praxis of destruction."[14]

The critical response to Serra's installation in Haus Lange was overwhelmingly positive. In a letter to Stockebrand, Berswordt-Wallrabe wrote that the exhibition was "the high point of all the exhibitions that have been carried out in Haus Lange to date," going even further to suggest that the installation remain intact in situ to serve as a distinguished exemplar of the anti-environment paradigm.[15] The notion that a "comprehensive praxis of destruction" could be so readily understood as profoundly compatible with its architectural context is noteworthy. Aesthetic legitimacy was conferred upon a condition that consisted of affirmation and negation operating within one artistic frame. Mies was affirmed by Serra who was countering Mies. As a synthetic work, which is the only way the installation can be considered, legitimacy was thereby conferred on a condition characterized not by any conventional notion of aesthetic coherence, but on one characterized by organized incoherence. Serra's installation was not seen to produce chaos or the cacophony of competing spatial/tectonic agendas. Rather, a curious sense of clarity was perceived to be granted to both the architecture and the sculpture. A new kind of middle condition was constituted, born of a proposition and its antithesis. This middle condition remained unnamed, but it was nonetheless apprehended and celebrated.

The history of architecture—and that of art as well—has not, by and large, shared this appreciation. The vast majority of architecture's history is written to acclaim conceptual, functional, and material commensurability, not the "muddled" condition formed by coexisting incompatibles. Perhaps this is the legacy of a basic Aristotelian premise that such a middle term is logically excluded. If found in the acts and minds of men, it is the product of compromise and weakness. The "environment/ anti-environment" paradigm asserts the possibility of *contradiction* as a possible praxis, and a powerful one.

In recent years it has become increasingly acceptable to see contradiction (sometimes rendered as the paradoxical) in Mies's Barcelona Pavilion and Villa Tugendhat and indeed as characteristic of the architect's work in general. This reading of Mies was not the received wisdom of the curators in Krefeld, nor the commentators of Serra's installation, nor, for that matter, of Serra himself. If it had been, it is possible that an entirely different reception would have figured in the Serra/Mies installation, which explicitly relied on a portrait of the architect that emphasized clarity, consistency, rationality, and tectonic coherence. The Mies that Serra countered was the Mies of rational methods.

Ironically, the architecture of the Krefeld villas seems significantly closer to that of the Barcelona Pavilion, equally preoccupied with a practice of ambiguity and discontinuity–a self-contained anti-environment. This claim is, in fact, one that we wish to make on behalf of Mies's Krefeld villas, albeit not with Serra's work as a counterfoil but as naked, vacant, free-standing environments. The architecture of the two Krefeld villas is, as it were, already preoccupied with its own self-denial. Both Haus Esters and Haus Lange are their own anti-environments. The architecture proposes certain spatial and structural conditions but simultaneously undermines them. The resulting "incoherence" is by design, and yields not chaos, but clarity.

The most extraordinary, although certainly not the only, example of this self-undoing in the Krefeld villas can be found precisely where it promises to do the most productive work–that is, in their structural conception. Bearing-wall structures have a few basic conditions that discipline architectural decisions. These are simple matters amounting to three basic rules that must be factored into the work at an early stage: first, bearing walls should not be punctured excessively; second, they should stack vertically to transfer loads; third, the placement of bearing walls is conditioned by the structure of the decking system.

Immediately obvious to the eye, and to all commentators on these villas, are the structural implications of the window openings on the south facades, with spans defying the conventions, and indeed the capacity, of bearing-wall structures. [6] The brickwork makes no visual concession to the openings; no lintels are indicated, no head conditions marked. Upon closer inspection, the bottom flange of a steel angle can be seen supporting the brick cladding. But the angle is only one of an otherwise invisible battery of steel members rallied to the support of the expansive window openings. The steel angle does not in fact span the window opening; it is suspended, strapped with flat steel bars to a steel channel above, which spans from jamb to jamb. A third member–a wide-flange beam–helps support the bearing wall above, and a fourth member–a stocky wide flange–transfers the floor load. Sandwiched within this array of beams is the barrel of the retractable shutter that blinds each window. [7, 8, 9]

The structural ensemble of the fenestration is the nexus of Kenneth Frampton's assessment of the villa's convoluted structural logic. Frampton notes:

[6]   Haus Lange, load-defying window spans
[7]   Haus Lange, window head detail
[8]   Hybrid structure revealed during restoration
[9]   Steel assembly over window opening

[6]

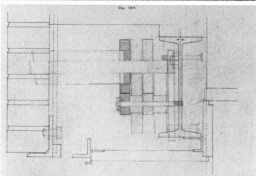

[7]

[8]

[9]

Mies's engineer, Ernst Walther, complained at length about the economic and technical problems involved in achieving such large spans in brick openings. In a letter to Mies, he complained of his liberal use of Reiner [sic] beams and other elaborate structural devices. However, such spans enabled Mies to provide large picture windows in both the Esters and Lange residences.[16]

Walther was not principally complaining about the structural feats involved in spanning the window openings. The incongruity of large sheets of glazing stretching horizontally across the exterior brick walls was not the only, or even the main, moment of structural gymnastics in the Krefeld villas. In fact, the Peiner beams referenced above are not associated with the difficulties caused by the fenestration. Peiner beams are steel sections characterized by markedly large flanges that are almost as wide as the beam's web is deep. They are strong, yet given their geometry, not particularly efficient. They are designed to conserve depth, but at the expense of massive self-weight. The liberal use of such members is a consequence of the fact that in both villas many large, eccentric loads are being transferred over long spans within a shallow structural depth. In other words, the Peiner beams draw our attention not to the windows, not to the condition of the periphery, but to a condition more central to the general character of the architecture, the overall structural status of these works. In Haus Lange there are sixteen concealed columns. In Haus Esters there are over 350 steel beams and over 50,000 kilograms (110,000 pounds) of steel.[17] The structural calculations for Haus Lange encompassed 88 pages; for Esters, an impressive 124.[18] As these figures suggest, these are not simple masonry structures. They are also not simple steel structures. They are complex hybrids presented, improbably, as simple brick structures.

Some of the structural complexity has to do with the scale of the spaces spanned. The main hall in Haus Lange measures 7 x 14 meters; clear-spanning even this short dimension required more than the usual domestic muscle. [10] (For comparison, the span between columns in Villa Tugendhat is just 4.9 meters.) But the length of the spans per se is not difficult to resolve structurally. Bearing-wall structures align space with structure; gravity imprints a line on the plan or through multiple plans, corresponding with, or rather sharing identity with, spatial demarcations. Erasing any substantial portion of such a line has a structural consequence, typically

[10] Haus Lange, seven-meter span in living room

[10]

marked by an architectural response: a transfer beam appears, a head condition thickens, or a column appears to announce the disruption of the tectonic logic. Removing the mark of gravity from the plan simply reinstates an equivalent mark on (or within) the ceiling. The best site for reading the tectonic logic of a bearing-wall structure is thus not the plan alone, but rather the plan and its reflection. This is precisely the opposite of a columnar structure, in which the meter of structure is divorced from the meter of enclosure: the sandwich of space between floor and ceiling is essentially unaffected by the meandering traces of enclosing surfaces. Erasing enclosure produces no structural echo.

The complexity in Haus Lange and Haus Esters arises from the desire to selectively erase gravity while suppressing the tectonic evidence of having done so. The principal site of this activity is within the horizontal stratum that separates the first and second floors, for this is a locus where numerous structural discontinuities are absorbed. Almost completely uninterrupted by dropped beams or headers over large passageways, the taut sheet of the first-floor ceilings in both villas conceals the fact that there are virtually no continuous interior bearing walls to support the roof loads. [11] The upper level of Lange in particular is populated with interior columns. The columns, however, do not align with bearing surfaces below, but rather bear down at rather inauspicious places—midway on the ceiling in the main hall, for example, or just a few centimeters from a bearing wall in Lange's dining room. Particularly in the case of the upper-floor bedroom/bathroom area, six columns carry a substantial load because the lowered roof over the bedroom corridor breaks the continuity of the roof beams.[19] Essentially, these columns carry half the roof load, and the north exterior masonry wall, with its continuous ribbon of clerestory windows, carries almost none. Weight is shifted away from a masonry wall and reallocated to columns that have no bearing surface below them. [12] Not surprisingly, the Peiner beams proliferate in the shallow zone under these columns, above the uninflected plaster plane of the ceiling in the living room. There is another massive vertical discontinuity at the perimeter, again in Haus Lange, again camouflaged by the continuity of the first-floor ceiling plane: the southeastern, second-floor corner floats in space. A serious collection of beams, squeezed into the shallow floor cavity, is rallied to transfer the load to the southeastern terrace wall, which itself rests directly above the 8-meter clear-span of the triple-car garage door. [13]

[11]   Zones of continuous bearing walls from roof to
        foundation: Haus Lange (left), Haus Esters (right)
[12]   Haus Lange, building section
[13]   Haus Esters, long span at garage

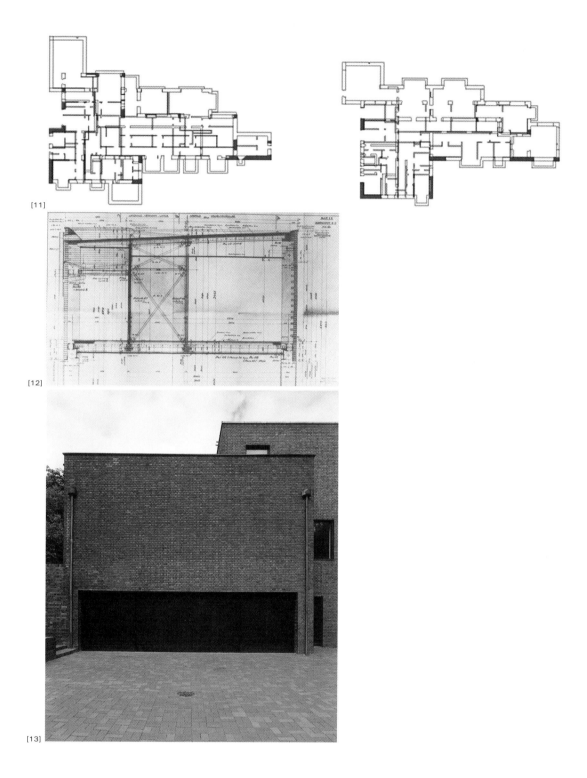

[11]

[12]

[13]

[14]

[14] Haus Esters, invisible transfer beams support garden facade above

[15] Haus Esters, expansive ceiling in living room supports columns above (Christopher Williams exhibit in background)

[15]

Similarly, more than half the length of the upper-level garden facade of Haus Esters has no load-bearing walls beneath it, nor are there any gestures indicating how its load is transferred or where it is transferred to. This facade floats above the volume of the woman's room and dining rooms below, and is underpinned by multiple transfer beams hidden by the now familiar unperturbed ceiling plane. [14] Four of the five interior columns that support a fair portion of the roof of Haus Esters bear down on spatial entities rather than on structural nodes, two of them resting directly over the living room with its sizable clear-span.[20] Again the loads are whisked away by transfer beams invisible to the eye. [15] The undoing of bearing-wall logic is massive and pervasive.

A more extreme demonstration of what might be called a rebuke of gravity occurs in the living room of each villa. Long, thick, and apparently continuous, the south wall of the living room of Lange (the situation in Esters is very similar) is one of the few moments on the main-level plans where dense matter is amassed with a degree of linear continuity. [16, 17] This wall is the line of support where many of the transfer beams mentioned above terminate and find bearing surface. The wall is approximately 7.5 meters long. At the bottom portion of this wall is a bookcase, a low horizontal wood unit measuring approximately 1.12 meters high by 5 meters in length, sheathed with sliding glass doors. [18] The bookcase is not on the wall, but recessed so that it consumes virtually the entire depth of the wall, the front face of the woodwork set perfectly flush with the wall's plaster finish. A small, 1.2-cm-wide reveal produces a thin shadow separating the plaster edge of the wall from the 3-cm-wide exposed edge of the casework. To maintain this narrow gap would require very precise craftsmanship; the effect is that of a razorlike cut into the white skin of the wall. Nothing about the design acknowledges that massive loads are bearing down from above. The white skin is unmarred. Structurally, a bearing wall has been erased for over three quarters of its original length, requiring, as elsewhere, the deployment of a transfer beam. This steel member is concealed within the wall thickness immediately above the bookcase. It can be seen on a drawing for the long horizontal casework in the woman's room, which is mounted on the opposite side of the wall in question. This casework is also recessed into the thickness of the wall, and detailed similarly but supported by bolts driven into a deep I-beam, the same beam that spans above the bookcase. This (mis)treatment of a bearing wall is, of course,

[16]   Haus Lange, bookcase built into structural wall
[17]   Haus Esters, bookcase built into structural wall
[18]   Haus Lange, living room bookcase detail
[19]   Haus Esters, preliminary ground-floor plan

[16]

[17]

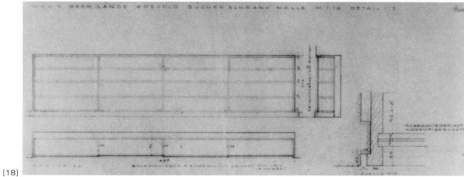

[18]

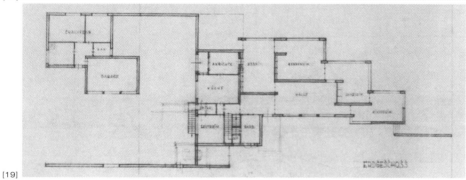

[19]

familiar, for it is directly analogous to that of the facade itself. Yet here it is more extreme. The horizontality of the bookshelf is exaggerated; its low, elongated form is more dogmatically incommensurate with the vertical voids permissible in bearing-wall structures. Furthermore, the wall that is thus undercut is not a minor structural moment, for it lies directly in line with the entire second-floor garden facade above and thus could have been one of the few structurally expedient arrangements. Because the hollowing of this wall occurs at the bottom, both the expanse of the ceiling and that of the wall itself appear to float. Weight is not merely dissipated as it is with the transfer beams hidden by the ceiling: it is shown first and then denied at the last moment any ground.

Most of the structural anomalies described above are the consequence of perverting the basic tectonic axioms of load-bearing systems. One seeks in vain for the conventional spatial logic and tectonic expression of bearing walls in both the elevations and the plans of each villa. An early scheme for Haus Esters makes it clear that Mies was not, however, simply pursuing a spatial paradigm (i.e. the free plan) with inappropriate structural means (i.e. bearing walls). The early plan has numerous thick walls and no sense of a free plan or of a desire for maximal transparency. [19] The outstanding and perplexing characteristic of this plan is that of the ten wall planes that comprise the main body of the plan, *no two align*. The precision with which the walls misalign is remarkable; sometimes it is a matter of only a few centimeters. Ten planes establish ten parallel but staggered trajectories. Each trace evaporates into space, into the void of a room or beyond, into the landscape. It is a plan utterly unconstrained by a basic principle: lines of bearing are spatially related to that which they structurally support, the roof or floor above. It is futile to try to imagine such a connection, for the plan is conceived as an open-air labyrinth, myriad thick walls with nothing but an ephemeral white sheet of plaster above. The decking would surely be a maze of steel, but which of these ten planes would actually carry transfer beams and which would not is impossible to decode, for the plan is designed to deny any structural hierarchy. The effect is a surplus of material but a lack of weight. By forcing gravity into untraceable pathways, weight itself becomes impossible to map.

In the Krefeld villas it is not possible to apprehend any spatial moment without simultaneously comprehending a material paradox; the two are inextricably

overleaf

[20]   Haus Esters, view from dining room to living room
and woman's room

linked. In this sense, the Krefeld villas align surprisingly well with recent observations regarding the German Pavilion's tectonic paradoxes: columns that negate their presence and walls that negate their nonstructural identity. It has, perhaps, been a mistake to characterize the Krefeld work as compromised, thereby focusing on a set of forces presumed to be external to the architect's method. More fruitful might be to accept a practice of ambiguity, of proposition and counter-proposition, as characteristic of both the villas in Krefeld and Mies himself. At stake here is, in fact, the question of canon formation; phrased more precisely, the question of canonical stability in the context of shifting evaluative ground. In the thinking of E. H. Gombrich, certain peaks of creative output exist not so much as consequences of critical judgments, but rather the other way around. According to Gombrich, critical judgments are formed and re-formed in order to come to grips with masterful creations; critical judgments do not masterpieces make. Gombrich has written that "as far as the peaks of art are concerned, it is not so much we who test the masterpiece, but the masterpiece which tests us."[21] To a degree, this explains the scholarly penchant for returning to the canonical well (i.e. the German Pavilion, Villa Tugendhat) even if it might be drier than other nearby sources. It explains why in the contemporary climate in which Mies is under reconstruction as everything but a rationalist, the iconic works remain the privileged source of evidence. If one believes, however, that masterpieces do not, and never did, simply announce themselves—that they are not simply and suddenly there, like clouds or rocks—then one might alternatively suggest that the paradoxical attributes of the Krefeld villas qualify them for consideration in a reconfigured understanding of Mies. Arguably, a shift in critical perspective should produce a corresponding shift in what is considered worthy of inclusion.

The situation with Mies is particularly sensitive to the question of which works are included, as it becomes increasingly difficult to point to anyone other than Mies to uphold certain central tenets of modernity itself. And here one has to acknowledge that the art installations which can serve as access to the Krefeld villas have at times rendered a disservice to the understanding of this architecture. The case of Richard Serra is one instance. Serra needed a stable Mies as a pendant for his unstable installations. But his slabs do more than prop themselves up; they simultaneously prop up a version of Mies that is, slowly, collapsing.

Windows and Other Weaknesses [1]

In 1552 the Flemish artist Pieter Aertsen painted *Transience Still Life* (*In the Background Christ with Mary and Martha*), [2] which depicts, at least in part, a well-known episode from the Gospel of St. Luke. Christ has entered the house of the sisters Mary and Martha. Mary takes her place at the feet of Christ to attend to his words; Martha, preoccupied by household chores, appeals to Christ to admonish Mary and bid her to help with the tasks. Jesus replies, "Martha, Martha, you are worried and distracted by many things; there is need of only one thing. Mary has chosen for the better part, which will not be taken away from her."[1] The biblical narrative is portrayed in knowing conformity with Alberti's rules for the depiction of *historia*: the human agents are acting out grand narratives; they are symmetrically framed; and they are situated with precise balance within rational space. As *historia*, Aertsen's painting is a failure.

It is a failure because the painting is consumed in large part by a profusion of earthly goods, stacked, spilling beyond the frame, a *natura morte* in a state of unstable equilibrium. The biblical scene—painted almost in grisaille—is relegated to the background and framed asymmetrically by the foreground scene, painted with the finest brush and the fullest palette. The foreground scene and its compositional imperatives is the exact opposite of the biblical scene and its compositional imperatives. Given this incongruity, the painting is not a mature still life, a genre that had yet to be born.

At the time of its conception, Aertsen's painting was criticized for its lack of consistency, for being stuck between representational modalities. It took several

[1]   Ernst Caramelle, *Untitled*, Museum Haus Lange, 1990

[1]

centuries to recognize that the painting's double weaknesses are in fact its singular strength. The obvious, intentional, and powerful splitting of the painterly surface appeared to eyes of Aertsen's contemporary critics as a lack of compositional resolution, a disciplinary flaw, a technical and conceptual weakness. To contemporary eyes, this pictorial incoherence—in which the representational strategies of one genre are framed by those of a second—is the heart of the work's ability to produce meaning. The entire semantic content of the painting resides in its duality: the still life recontextualizes the biblical depiction, sets the sacred narrative against the profane universe, and establishes relationships between the two depictions that constitute the painting's iconology: between the leg of lamb and the Christ figure, between the world of the flesh and the world of the spirit, and between the lump of unleavened bread and Christ's incarnation.

By surrounding a *historia* with a *nature morte*, the work interrogates the art of painting; "painting" is framed by painting. It is precisely the split in the image that prevents the work from being consumed by its narrative. The structural "weaknesses" force the viewer to keep one eye on the artifice of the painting itself. The power of the image and the creative contribution of the artist relies precisely on the work's internal conflicts. Aersten makes us receptive to the possibility that formal incongruence, skillfully balanced, can be a device for making visible and problematizing a given discipline's conventions.

Mies's two villas in Krefeld need to be seen with precisely such sensitivity in order to yield their significance. If one assumes that Mies was attempting to produce aesthetically modern but typologically conventional brick structures, the villas are clearly failures. If one assumes that Mies was trying to produce an entirely new typology, they also fail. Both assumptions characterize the manner in which these buildings have been received, and the clearest example of this approach is the critical reception of the villas' windows. Indeed, they are undeniably problematic. They are too large for traditional bearing-wall construction, yet too small to sustain a fully modern architectural expression. They have thus served as the nexus for the case that these are Mies's most "compromised" works. Stuck in a masonry world, one is told, the generous but conventional fenestration offers a view to a horizon where Barcelona and Tugendhat are already taking shape. In their own terms, they document a failure.

[2]   Pieter Aertsen, *Transience Still Life (In the Background Christ with Mary and Martha)*, 1552

[3]   Mies with early pastel sketch

[2]

[3]

To be fair, the failure was never presented as a lack of creative ability on the part of the architect. As testimony to the potency of Mies's vision in 1928, we are repeatedly presented with the early pastel perspective of Haus Esters showing the garden facade with a nearly full-height, mullionless glass membrane wrapping the volume of the house. So familiar is the photograph of Mies standing in front of this drawing, pastel in hand, it may well be better known than the built work itself. [3] As to the clarity of Mies's intentions, we are offered his proclamation, "I wanted to make this house much more in glass."[2] And to Mies's ability to execute his vision, we are reminded of the almost simultaneous production of the German Pavilion, followed closely by Villa Tugendhat. In other words, we are told, Mies was creatively ready and technically able to break entirely new ground in Krefeld, if only circumstances had permitted, if only the clients had cooperated.

It is unclear, however, whether or not *that* kind of new ground was what Mies intended in Krefeld. *That* kind, of course, refers to the development of the glass-enclosing wall, the complete and clear separation of bearing and enclosing functions, material expression of structural rationality, and the uninhibited extension of the interior to the exterior. Mies said he wanted to realize that kind of architecture in Krefeld, and he sketched that kind of architecture in the preliminary elevation. But he did not build it. Historic records shed some light, albeit inconclusively, on why not.

On October 4, 1928, Josef Esters wrote a letter to his business partner, Hermann Lange, summarizing various unresolved issues concerning their houses.[3] A good portion of the letter focused on the windows. Clearly, the size of the windows had been, and still was, a topic of much discussion among the principals involved in the project.[4] In a wonderful testament to the force of the mundane, the principal featured in Ester's letter was less Architekt Mies, but rather Herr Hochkramer, purveyor of heat exchangers: the radiators, it seems, were the problem. The large areas of single-pane glazing demanded larger than usual radiators to compensate for the heat loss. Three times Esters, who accepted responsibility for overseeing the construction of both villas, had broached the subject of lowering the sill heights of the windows. Apparently the third effort to coax them below 58 centimeters—whether on Mies's insistence, Lange's, or his own is not clear—triggered an ultimatum from Herr Hochkramer. If the sills were lower than 58 centimeters, the radiators would no longer fit properly beneath them, leaving only two options: they would have to be placed in a wall cavity elsewhere in the room, or they would have to project beyond the sill if placed below the window.

In response to this ultimatum, there was apparently a directive from Mies: any projecting or exposed heating units were out of the question. In fact, so important was the elimination of any projecting or visible radiators, Esters actually outlined for Lange the option of increasing the exterior wall thickness simply to increase the available niche depth. The resulting area of the room, of course, would be reduced by the same amount that the wall was thickened; to compensate for this loss in usable space, Esters explored the logical yet absurd solution of enlarging the footprint of the entire villa. Alternatively, the radiators could be placed in niches in the fragments of the available bearing wall next to the windows, although the large windows had reduced the amount of wall to a bare minimum. This solution would surely have required an increase in bearing wall—ergo, a reduction in the proportion of glazing. Ironically, smaller radiators would then have probably been sufficient after all. Esters closes his letter with an eminently wise and quotable observation: "I must confess that I had not imagined that the modern way of building would result in such technical complications."[5]

The point of recounting this episode, aside from a certain wry pleasure in witnessing what the late architecture theorist Jan Turnovsky identified as architecture's heroic failure when faced with weight and thickness,[6] is to suggest that maximizing the glazing was not the priority in these works, at least not by October 1928. Conspiring to make infrastructure vanish was a priority, however, and this vanishing act pertains not just to the environmental controls, but to support mechanisms of all stripes—structural, mechanical, functional, and even gravitational. One can list numerous moves ("technical complications") that contribute to this architecture's particular quality: a convoluted structural system, a cladding system more concerned with pattern consistency than tectonic veracity, unarticulated fenestration, and now the preference for recessed radiators over increased glazing. [4]

A strategy emerges, but it is not a strategy that points backward to the preliminary drawing. Whatever early visions Mies may have entertained for the Krefeld houses, it is clearly myopic to insist on measuring the built work against an early sketch. Mies himself had moved on. Almost nothing in the built work aligns itself with the project that many wish Mies had pursued; even very, *very* large windows would have done nothing to change the fact that these are bearing-wall, and not columnar, structures. There is every reason to assume that what Mies wanted with respect to the windows in Haus Lange and Haus Esters, and with respect to this architecture in general, was pretty much what he got. Mies configured these buildings—these windows—well within the confines of conventionality, rather than at the limits, in order not to break free or declare limits but, on the contrary, to explore the core. In other words, the windows frame the category "window" without resorting to the complete demolition of the category. They achieve sufficient distance from the window's traditional role as mere openings in walls and simultaneously offer resistance to the radical recategorization of "window" associated with the glass walls/frame construction of high modernism.

The proof for this speculation is evidenced by omission. Nowhere, in the thirty corners that are offered by the two villas, does Mies choose the device popularized by Walter Gropius in 1914 (Fagus Factory), by Gerrit Rietveld in 1924 (Schröder House), by Le Corbusier in 1928 (Villa Stein), and by countless other modernists well before 1928: the corner window. Given the extravagant use of steel in both villas, removing a few—or even a few dozen—brickwork corners would have been the least of Mies's structural contrivances. Without adding a single square foot of glass, a simple shifting of the fenestration away from a position of equipoise surrounded by brickwork to a position of dramatic anti-structuralism would have rendered the facades of Haus Lange and Haus Esters more aggressively modern. It would have at least demonstrated the maximal extent to which a bearing-wall structure could be like a columnar structure. The polemical character of such an effort is both familiar to modernity and what we have come to expect of this architect. The fact that Mies did not deploy or even explore this option suggests that the maintenance of some essential "windowness"—a void in a wall—had a value and purpose.

This value and purpose, however, seems not to have been the obvious, namely viewing. The south- and west-facing windows are of approximately equal size, but their views are of distinctly unequal quality. To the south from both villas is a deep vista of lawn and trees stretching to the then unbuilt horizon of fields, framed by picturesquely grouped chestnut trees. [5] To the west, the view from Esters is of the working quarters of Lange, from Lange, the side of the neighboring villa. If the windows

[4]   Radiator concealed beneath window

[5]   Haus Esters, view to garden

[6]   Haus Esters, staggered massing and folded views

[4]

[5]

[6]

were intended to offer a west-to-south panorama, the "viewed" certainly does not reciprocate the gesture. As viewing frames, as forms hinting at how they are to be appropriated, the fenestration is strangely mute in terms of organizing the landscape beyond into a hierarchical schema. In this conventional sense of viewing and viewed, the view out is undisciplined, generous yet unsatisfying, like an incomplete invitation. Unless, however, one does not look *out* and *beyond* the windows, but rather *through* and *at* them.

It is possible to look through and at the windows because of the peculiar arrangement of the south facades of the villas. In fact, it is difficult not to be seduced by this unique optical opportunity. Commentators have noted in word and image the staggered articulation of the rear of both villas and the accordion-like arrangement of windows this allows. [6] This feature has been understood as Mies's attempt to forge an interlocking relationship with the exterior. Barry Bergdoll remarks that in Haus Lange and Haus Esters,

> the garden facade develops the theme of the progressive stepping forward
> of the building mass to provide maximum exposure to the garden and land-
> scape, while the garden responds, intermeshed with the facade almost like
> the cogs of a gear.... [I]ndividual windows of these houses frame landscape
> views so large as to be essentially brought indoors.[7]

But to "telescope out" (Bergdoll's term) spaces several yards out into the garden, with each space granted its own oversized opening, does not bring nature closer. Indeed, given the emphatically blocklike massing, one can almost read the stepped volumes as extending the built body into the landscape so as to *defer* nature, like an advancing army unit securing territory with each southward step. This stepping pattern produces more than a few pronounced consequences in terms of the plan. What seems obvious from the perspective of massing—namely that each outward step would correspond to the width of a room—turns out not to be the case at all. Each step is about half a room in length, resulting in a number of curiously L-shaped rooms—a nested, puzzlelike, staggered plan configuration and a building mass that camouflages, rather than clarifies, the internal workings of the plan. The staggering willfully introduces a multitude of orthogonal displacements.

Thus the staggered massing acts to defer nature, and the resulting large windows facing in two directions do not correspond to a view. So perhaps this is not so much an architecture that reaches out into nature, but one that folds back onto itself; likewise, it is not a fenestration system that frames nature, but one that frames itself. [7] The resulting view is not perpendicular to the window frame but oblique to the glazed surface: a folded view. The viewing subject is split between the option of viewing directly outward or viewing at an angle to the "picture" frame. This oblique view is frequently framed to the power of two, sometimes even to the power of three, and in one instance in Haus Lange, to the power of five. A view of a view of a view of a view of a view of the garden: can one really call this a view of the garden? It is always an image, a representation, a picture. Frames interfere, frames are framed; like Aertsen's painting, frames are situated within a framed condition. Nature is framed, window frames are framed, nature framed in a window frame is framed. This view might well be the principal aesthetic achievement of the buildings.

Can one reasonably assert that the Krefeld villas were shaped in large part to give life to a view of this kind? The very notion that a view oblique to a frame is a legitimate entity requires some justification. The trope of the window-as-picture has, since Alberti, assumed a set of orthogonal relationships between viewer, frame, and viewed subject. The implications of the Albertian model for both painting and architecture has spawned an entire field of study, so-called "Cartesian perspectivalism."[8] The view of an Albertian painting, or from Alberti's window, implies a fixed subject armed with steady and clear vision, exercising surveillance and control, and isolated from the material world from which he is ultimately and consciously superior. In this model, the oblique view is typically posited as illicit, as a distortion. The sideways look, the fragmentary view, the ill-framed composition, the glance rather than the gaze, the disorientating reflections caused by tilted glass versus the penetrating clarity of the open window: these characteristics are not part of the Albertian-Cartesian visual model. With few exceptions, there is no extensive history of the oblique view.

One such exception is that of the "curious perspective," the anamorphosis.[9] In anamorphic constructions, an image is revealed only when the viewer engages a work from an unfamiliar vantage point or deploys a device such as a curved mirror or a special eyepiece. The resulting image is fragile and flitters away and back again with each subtle movement of the observer. What is revealed by this arrangement is not just the image itself but the laws and techniques by which representations are constructed. The artifice of representation is as much the subject of the anamorphosis as is the particular figure or object that rewards the viewer's labor, for the beholder must work to experience the image. Alberti's perspective has become "naturalized" to the point where its artifice is no longer visible. The artifice of representation disappears into the simulation of reality.[10] The anamorphosis is thus the "unnatural" twin of Alberti's ideal, for the device that renders the anamorphosis visible is explicitly, as in the case of convex or concave mirrors, present. When Charles Baudelaire, in *The Parisian Prowler*, writes, "He who looks outside through a window open never sees as much as he who looks at a window closed,"[11] one cannot help but think that it is the reflective nature of glass that, by interfering with clear vision, produces awareness of the separation of viewer from view and, by mirroring the viewer viewing, adds to the view beyond. The reflection imposes self-awareness.

To return to Mies's zigzagging windows, we can place them outside the Albertian paradigm and somewhere amidst Aertsen's frames-within-frames, within the experience of the anamorphic image, and among Baudelaire's reflective windowpanes. The common denominator of these latter visual models is that views are offered only in conjunction with a delay. The delay is produced by including (assertively and positively) the viewing framework within the view; the intervening framework opens an opportunity to contemplate the viewing machinery itself as the producer of the view. The diagonal views through the lower-level windows in Haus Lange and Haus Esters function in this fashion and produce this form of contemplation.

Such complex visual experiences are not limited to the windows alone; there is a consistency of method that extends to the interior as well. To understand how the interior produces this effect, it is helpful to turn again to an artist who intimately engaged the Krefeld houses. In 1990, the Austrian artist Ernst Caramelle exhibited in Haus Lange. For the lower level, he produced a series of small paintings, and on the dining room wall, a large mural, all inspired by the interior of Haus Lange. The mural is worth our attention. [see 1] It is composed primarily of L-shaped fields of tone with a single rectangular insert. The composition is resolutely asymmetrical. Despite the flatness of the fields of tone, the panels have a definite sense of depth, not the kind produced by perspectival elements, but the depth implied by overlapping planes. The

[7]   Haus Esters, diagonal view (to the power of four)

mural is delimited at the top by the plaster ceiling and at the bottom by the wooden baseboard. The left and right edges of the mural suggest an arbitrary cutoff, as if the unpainted white plaster wall were delimiting our view of a more complete vista beyond. In fact, the mural is carefully positioned so as to incorporate the left-hand portion of the untouched plaster wall intimately into the overall composition. For only if one includes this portion of the wall does the image form an asymmetrical but balanced whole with the dark rectangle at its approximate geometric center. It is not easy to know exactly where one should stand to view this image.

Caramelle's mural does not, as far as we can establish, depict any particular view, but it nonetheless offers a compelling interpretation of the villa. They are linked to the architecture not by color or implied materiality, but by a particular conception of a view that permeates the interior of both villas. They are performative rather than representational, acting as a form of analysis. Caramelle's paintings instruct us to observe the alignments of doors and openings and views. With few exceptions, the openings on the ground floors of both houses are situated so as not to align with, or be centered on, any other opening. [8] The single exception in Haus Esters is the pair of doors between the children's room and the woman's room. The single exception in Haus Lange is the pair of doors between the woman's room and the dining room.

The disposition of these doorways in Lange is the analytic subject of Caramelle's mural. For when viewed from the woman's room through the pair of heavily trimmed door embrasures, Caramelle's mural assumes a second reading: it is an extension of these two doorways, a trompe l'oeil of sorts. [9] The right edge of the yellow field aligns with the right doorjambs and the left edge of the yellow field aligns with the left doorjambs. The recessive yellow field is the exact width of the two doorways and the top of this field is at their exact head height. The yellow field is thus a doorway, with the dark area at the bottom of the mural functioning as an extension of the floor plane, and the black rectangle is a distant, windowlike void. But the mural is not an extension or reinforcement of this miniature enfilade—the only enfilade—in Haus Lange. It is rather an assault on the logic of this and all enfilades, for the frames of the aligned doors are in no way a frame for the mural. The mural only feigns compliance with the doorframes as if to acknowledge this classically constructed view only to deny its authority. The mural slips out to the left; the image as framed by the two doorways excludes a substantial portion of the painting and

[8]   Haus Lange, nonaligned doorways

[9]   Caramelle's mural viewed through
      doorways, Museum Haus Lange, 1990

[8]

[9]

includes a fragment of raw canvas, the naked plaster wall. Views and frames have declared their independence.

Such independence is a subtle but palpable characteristic of both villas. Most emphatically, doors and passages do not align themselves with the windows. Given that the houses are understood as cellular, it is surprising that these plans yield up a large variation of vistas across multiple thresholds. These vistas of misaligned openings are reinforced by the wood molding that outlines the bases of the walls and the heads and jambs of the openings. This molding is highly graphic and slyly orna- mental. It consists of a wide band of dark oak trim with its grain consistently ori- ented vertically, even in horizontal applications. It courses throughout the houses like an austere but stylish appliqué, a dark piping embellishing the white fabric of the interior.

As mentioned before, immense effort and expense was incurred to allow open- ings without visible headers and to provide a smooth ceiling despite vast eccentric forces overhead. Yet having vanquished beams, Mies applies trim. A seamless visual flow between spatial units was clearly not the intent. Nor were completely autonomous cells. Openings are outlined with a highly visible, albeit abstract line, as if to underscore the very lack of actual structural members. [10] Window jambs and heads are rendered with the same trim and are thereby incorporated into the overall system. The windows therefore neither disappear as unmarked voids, nor do they appear as conventionally framed "pictures" against a wall. Like so many other ele- ments in this architecture, they are suspended between states. Walls, doorways, pas- sageways and windows are all gathered together under the sign of a single abstract cipher. As this cipher tracks through the villas, it describes a set of receding inverted U's that appear almost like reflections in a skewed mirror. [11] The U's do not line up. Despite the rather conventional nature of the volumetric units, Lange and Esters achieve a spatial dynamic simply by misaligning the joints between these units and celebrating this misalignment by marking the joints with contrasting trim. In photo- graphs of the interior, this displacement often makes it appear that the photographer is positioned slightly off-axis. In fact, there is no other position, as Caramelle ably demonstrates.

In writing about Aertsen's painting, the semiotician-cum-art theorist, Victor Stoichita, termed such works "genuine theoretical objects."[12] By this he meant to

[10]   Haus Esters, trim tracks
[11]   Haus Esters, receding nonaligned doorways

[10]

[11]

define an art-historical genre whose subject is its own disciplinary conventions. Stoichita characterizes Aertsen's canvas as "paintings whose theme is painting." Such projects have the strange condition of being both novel and retrospective. They are novel only in their treatment of their discipline's past. If, as we have attempted to demonstrate, Mies's two Krefeld villas are such "genuine theoretical objects," it is not surprising that they caused consternation among those critics anxious to see Mies as the standard-bearer for modernity. Modern projects are original and prospective by definition; they are original to the degree that they set forth the conditions for their discipline's future.

Perhaps the only truly forward-looking aspect of Mies's Krefeld villas can be found in Haus Lange. There, the two large south-facing window panes—in the man's study and the drawing room, respectively—are outfitted with motorized mechanisms that lower the vast glass sheets into the basement at the push of a button mounted on the window jamb. These windows fall into the category of original and prospective entities, inventive prototypes that would be deployed to great effect in Villa Tugendhat, where the window as such is effectively destroyed. In contrast to Haus Lange, the south-facing windows in Haus Esters are conventional casement windows, or rather not entirely conventional, for the hardware was thoughtfully redesigned to allow the multiple large, metal-framed glass lights to lie absolutely flush on one another, yielding a delicacy and strength unattainable by conventional wood frame elements. [12] The windows in Esters fall perfectly into the category of the novel and the retrospective. It is a sign of enormous talent when even a window hinge can be rendered as a genuine theoretical entity.

[12]   Haus Esters, folding steel windows

overleaf
[13]   View from Haus Lange to Haus Esters

[12]

Conclusion
Architecture, Acting

A remarkable number of artists and artworks have worked in and on Haus Esters and Haus Lange since the early 1960s, yielding a unique legacy at the intersection of contemporary art and modern architecture. Yet the perceptions and reactions to Mies's architecture have been anything but concordant. For example, artist Zvi Goldstein perceived the villas as "refreshing landmarks of modesty and simplicity," while conversely, Maria Eichhorn observed that "the large spaces (halls) were planned by the architect and his clients in the grand style."[1] British painter Alan Charlton declared that Haus Esters, with its clear, rectangular, light-filled spaces and multiple balconies and terraces, exemplified the ideals of the modern international style. [2] On the other hand, Coosje van Bruggen described Haus Esters as "autumnal," and Katharina Fritsch concluded that Haus Lange performed best in the rain (her proposed sculpture was an artificial rain cloud). [1] Photographer Andreas Gursky praised the semicellular plan of Haus Lange, which suited his preference for displaying photographs individually, while the installation artist Joe Scanlon was impressed by the cinematic quality of the same interior.

To be sure, certain features of the villas—the windows in particular—surface with regularity as common ground for a number of artists, but the resultant installations tend to expand rather than consolidate the status of the architecture. For example, Mies—and Mies historians—may have desired more glass, but many artists recoiled from the perceived overexposure: Jannis Kounellis walled up selective windows with blackened rocks, providing patches of calculated darkness; [3, 4] Christo and Jeanne-Claude obscured the windows with translucent brown paper, providing entire rooms

[1]   Katharina Fritsch, *Cloud*, 1987

[1]

of pure diffuse radiance. [5, 6] Even Mies's design method sponsored varied reactions. Daniel Buren detected evidence of serial production in the twinned structures, and superimposed the plan of Lange over that of Esters to concretize the precise variations between the two. [7, 8] Michael Asher also detected rational planning in the villas, but superimposed the plan of Haus Lange, rotated by 90 degrees, onto itself, demonstrating not the rational but rather the aleatory consequences of operational logic. [9, 10]

Like the original occupants, the artists who dwelled in the villas arrived with predetermined and diverse habits, and the architecture seems to have satisfied a remarkable range of desires. Yet this architecture is never one with those desires or, put otherwise, is one with many different desires. The villas are both brooding yet light-filled; the windows both large yet too small; the scale of the villas is indeed grand, yet they are devoid of traditional signs of pomp; the rooms are discrete, yet the views are sweeping; and both the original Biedermeier and the imported Mies furniture seem equally at home. In other words, the villas are easily inhabited because they are received as underdetermined.

This might seem to be an unlikely statement about a set of buildings by Mies van der Rohe, an architect who designed structures notoriously difficult to inhabit precisely because they were overdetermined. But the Krefeld villas are not anomalies; in fact, the complex architectural strategy of opposing propositions employed by Mies in Krefeld is very similar to the strategy used in Barcelona or in Brno or in White Plains. What makes the Krefeld villas unique—as formal artifacts and as technical challenges—is the conventional vocabulary to which the strategy is applied. What makes the villas so attractive as subjects of study and as sites for dwelling is the speed with which this strategy is disclosed.

Haus Lange and Haus Esters are surely Mies's slowest projects. Many visits, sustained attention, and perhaps even dwelling are required to appreciate that these solid structures are slowly dissolving into a maze of contradictions, that their stability is a ruse. The buildings are intended to be apprehended analytically, not viscerally. The artist Bethan Huws observed that "you cannot feel anything here, it's a place that thinks."[2] There is certainly very little in the Krefeld work that compares to the immediate, overwhelming sensuality of Mies's iconic projects. The Krefeld approach decidedly eschews aesthetic absorption; nowhere in Krefeld is one offered the kind of oceanic experience Herr Tugendhat had before his wall of veined onyx.[3]

[2]   Alan Charlton, *8 Elements* (foreground), Museum
Haus Esters, 1991–92

[2]

And no one can maintain, as Robin Evans does for Barcelona, that Haus Lange and Haus Esters open up a therapeutic aesthetic amnesia via the gripping force of beauty in order to hold the world at bay;[4] the Krefeld villas offer no such escape. Bricks, white walls, wood trim: could the sensual appetite be offered much less in the way of material distraction?

Mies's tactic in Krefeld is similar to that perfected by playwright Bertolt Brecht, who famously insisted that his audience be held at an emotional distance from his performances (no reverie here), that an awareness of "actors-acting" be maintained to prevent the audience from lapsing into a state of absorption. Brecht demanded the mental participation of his audience, not only after the performance, but during it. We know that in order to produce this effect, Brecht's ensemble had to be untrained.[5] They had to learn to acknowledge the audience as audience, to occasionally miss perfect pitch while singing a Kurt Weill number while communicating to the audience that the miss was deliberate and thus not a miss at all. They were trained to wink. Brecht would not permit his audience to forget the unnaturalness of the stage. Only in this way, Brecht argued, could the theater of the stage actually become ontologically engaged with (become as real as) the theater of life.

There is a great deal of what we might call architectural "untraining" in the Krefeld villas, perhaps enough to dispel the notion that Mies's childhood experiences on building sites were all too formative. Contrivances and dissonances are distributed throughout the villas, vying for a piece of the dweller's attention. Mies, nudging at the participants in their domestic routine, wishes to remind them of the artifice, the unnaturalness, of their surroundings. Unnaturalness, of course, is the precondition for architecture; it is what makes architecture, as opposed to the beaver's dam, a cultural enterprise. The various contrivances that we have outlined stimulate an awareness of many architectural elements that have been, as it were, naturalized through appropriation by everyday use. What makes the situation in Krefeld so provocative, and what makes it interesting as an alternate modern paradigm, is precisely its proximity to practices that have taken on the character of the natural. Bricks, windows, trimwork, gravity: these are the characters that play on Mies's stage. We recognize them as familiar types, perhaps at first too familiar, even a bit uninteresting; costumed in more or less everyday garb, they are certainly not spectacular, just normal.

And then, quite distinctly, they wink.

[3]   Jannis Kounellis, *Untitled*, Museum Haus Esters, 1984

[4]   Kounellis, *Untitled*, Museum Haus Esters, 1984

[5]   Christo wraps Museum Haus Lange, 1971

[6]   Christo and Jeanne-Claude, *Wrapped Floors—Wrapped Walkways*, Museum Haus Lange, 1971

[7]   Daniel Buren, *Plan contre-plan, travail in situ*, Museum Haus Esters, 1982

[8]   Buren, *Plan contre-plan, travail in situ*, Museum Haus Esters, 1982

[9]   Michael Asher, *Rotated Plan*, Museum Haus Lange, 1982

[10] Asher, *Rotated Plan*, Museum Haus Lange, 1982

[3]

[4]

[5]

[6]

[7]

[8]

[9]

[10]

Notes

Introduction: Notes on Almost Nothing

1 H. T. Cadbury-Brown, "Ludwig Mies van der Rohe: An Address of Appreciation," *Architectural Association Journal* 75, no. 834 (July–August 1959): 26–46. Mies's statement on page 31 continues: "He [Lange] was the president of the silk industry in Germany, but that was to his sorrow. He drank a lot of wine, and so on. That is what you get."

2 Schulze, *Mies van der Rohe: A Critical Biography* (Chicago: University of Chicago Press, 1985), 145, 147 (photo).

3 Haus Lange was exhibited at the Museum of Modern Art in the 1932 Modern Architecture—International Exhibition and again in the 1947 Mies van der Rohe retrospective.

4 Johnson, *Mies van der Rohe* (New York: Museum of Modern Art, 1947), 206.

5 Jan Maruhn and Nina Senger, "Two Villas," in *Ein Ort fur Kunst/A Place for Art: Ludwig Mies van der Rohe, Haus Lange–Haus Esters*, ed. Julian Heynen (Krefeld: Krefelder Kunstmuseen and Verlag Gerd Hatje, 1995), 13.

6 Johnson, *Mies van der Rohe*, 206.

7 Bill, *Ludwig Mies van der Rohe* (Milano: Il Balcone, 1955), 33.

8 Hilberseimer, *Mies van der Rohe* (Chicago: Paul Theobald and Company, 1956); Blake, *Mies van der Rohe: Architecture and Structure* (Baltimore: Penguin Books, 1964), 37.

9 Blaser, *Mies van der Rohe* (New York: Praeger Publishers, 1965).

10 Tegethoff, *Mies van der Rohe: die Villen und Landhausprojekte* (Essen: R. Bacht, 1981). English translation by Russell M. Stockman, *Mies van der Rohe: the Villas and Country Houses* (New York: Museum of Modern Art, 1985).

11 Schulze, *Mies van der Rohe: A Critical Biography*, 144–47; Spaeth, *Mies van der Rohe* (New York: Rizzoli, 1985), 56–57; Frank Russell, ed., *Mies van der Rohe: European Works* (London: Academy Editions; New York: St. Martin's Press, 1986), 58–61; Cohen, *Mies van der Rohe*, trans. Maggie Rosengarten (London and New York: E & FN Spon, 1996), 50–51.

12 Frampton, "Mies van der Rohe: Avant-Garde and Continuity," in *Studies in Tectonic Culture: The Poetics of Construction in Nineteenth and Twentieth Century Architecture* (Cambridge, Mass.: MIT Press, 1995), 163–67.

13 Heynen, *Ein Ort für Kunst/A Place for Art*.

14 Heynen, *Ein Ort der denkt: Haus Lange und Haus Esters von Ludwig Mies van der Rohe: Moderne Architektur und Gegenwartskunst/A Place That Thinks: Haus Lange and Haus Esters by Ludwig Mies van der Rohe: Modern Architecture and Contemporary Art* (Krefeld: Krefelder Kunstmuseen, 2000).

15 Riley and Bergdoll, eds., *Mies in Berlin* (New York: Museum of Modern Art, 2001), 220–27.

16 Frampton, "Mies van der Rohe: Avant-Garde and Continuity," 167. See also Tegethoff, *Mies van der Rohe: The Art of Structure* (New York: Praeger, 1965), 21–23.

17 See Werner Blaser, *Mies van der Rohe: The Villas and Country Houses*, 63.

18 Gombrich, "Art History and the Social Sciences," in *Ideals and Idols: Essays on Values in History and in Art* (Oxford: Phaidon, 1979), 136.

19 Evans, "Mies van der Rohe's Paradoxical Symmetries," in *Translations from Drawing to Building and Other Essays* (Cambridge, Mass.: MIT Press, 1997), 241.

20 See, for example, Evans, "Mies van der Rohe's Paradoxical Symmetries," and Caroline Constant, "The Barcelona Pavilion as Landscape Garden: Modernity and the Picturesque," *AA Files* 20 (Autumn 1990): 46–54; and Jose Quetglas, "Fear of Glass: The Barcelona Pavilion," in *Architecture Production*, ed. Beatriz Colomina (New York: Princeton Architectural Press, 1988), 122–51.

21 Information on Hermann Lange is drawn largely from Jan Maruhn, "Bauherr der Moderne: Der Krefelder Seidenfabrikant Hermann Lange und sein Architekt Ludwig Mies van der Rohe, 1926–1938," (Ph.D diss., Magister Artium, Freie Universität Berlin, 1996); Maruhn and Senger, "Two Villas," 7–19.

22 Francesco Dal Co, *Figures of Architecture and Thought: German Architecture Culture, 1880–1920* (New York: Rizzoli, 1990), 172.

23 Tegethoff, *Mies van der Rohe: The Villas and Country Houses*, 61.

24 Maruhn and Senger, "Hermann Lange—Patron of Modernism," in Heynen, *Ein Ort für Kunst/A Place for Art*, 17.

25 Elaine S. Hochman, *Architects of Fortune: Mies van der Rohe and the Third Reich* (New York: Weidenfeld & Nicolson, 1989), 58–59. Hochman makes this claim without citing evidence. Maruhn in turn cites Hochman. See Maruhn, "Bauherr der Moderne," 21 n. 95.

26 Maruhn, "Bauherr der Moderne," 26.

27 A. Spelberg, *Gartendenkmalpflegerische Bearbeitung der Gärten Haus Lange/Haus Esters* (Krefeld: Stadt Krefeld-Grünflächenamt, 1992), 16, 18.

28 Julian Heynen, conversation with authors, Krefeld, Germany, September 20–21, 1995.

29 The term "minimal art" is often considered to have originated in the essay of the same name. See Richard Wollheim, "Minimal Art," *Arts Magazine* (January 1965). By 1995, the identification of Mies's architecture with minimalism had reached the point where it could be contested. See Rosalind Krauss, "The Grid, the /Cloud/, the Detail," and Ignasi de Solá-Morales Rubió, "Mies van der Rohe and Minimalism," in *The Presence of Mies*, ed. Detlef Mertins (New York: Princeton Architectural Press, 1994), 133–47, 149–55.

Klein's kleine Kammer

1 See (Justus) B(ier), "Kann man im Haus Tugendhat wohnen?" in *Die Form* VI, 10 (October 1931): 392–93; and Alice T. Friedman, *Women and the Making of the Modern House: A Social and Architectural History* (New York: Harry N. Abrams, Inc., 1998), 126–59.

2 "One speaks so often of the hostility of the new domestic architecture to pictures. The settlement at the Weissenhof in Stuttgart appears to support such a thesis. A few glances at the interior, which we are permitted

to reproduce here for the first time thanks to the cooperation of the architect, serve to undermine it." Walter Cohen, "Haus Lange in Krefeld," *Museum der Gegenwart* 1, no. 4 (1930–31): 162. Translation by the authors.

3 Yves Klein, *Conference de la Sorbonne*, June 3, 1959, as quoted in Gilbert Perlein and Bruno Cora, eds., *Yves Klein: Long Live the Immaterial* (New York: Delano Greenidge Editions, 2000), 222. In 1958, Klein collaborated with architect Walter Ruhnau to produce a scheme for a "pneumatic" architecture consisting of subterranean bedrooms, bathroom, and kitchen, with an open dwelling space above ground "enclosed" and climatized only by a constant blast of directed pressurized air. Sketches of this and fire and water architectures were included in the Krefeld exhibition. The projects are described in Udo Kulturmann, *Dynamische Architektur* (Munich: Lucas Cranach Verlag, 1959), 72–75.

4 Julian Heynen, ed., *Yves Klein: Monochrome und Feuer, Krefeld, 1961* (Krefeld: Krefelder Kunstmuseen and Buchhandlung Walter König, 1994), 3. This book is a comprehensive documentation of the genesis and development of Klein's 1961 exhibition in Haus Lange.

5 Ibid., 7.

6 Ibid., 9.

7 The drawing with notes is located in the Kaiser Wilhelm Museum Archive, Krefeld, Germany. Translation by the authors.

8 Heynen, *Yves Klein*, 6.

9 Jean-Marc Poinsot, "Two Exhibitions of Yves Klein" in Perlein and Cora, *Yves Klein: Long Live the Immaterial*, 47.

10 In a text entitled "Les cinq salles" ("The Five Rooms") printed in Klein's *Dimanche 27 Novembre 1960*, Klein describes a hypothetical exhibition/event that includes "passage into the void room, entirely immaculate white (including the floor) (IKI) (2)." In the same text, he decodes IKI as "(2)IKI 'equals' International Klein Immaterial (void)." See Poinsot, "Two Exhibitions of Yves Klein," 47. Klein's 1960 text is widely considered to be a precursor to the Krefeld exhibition. See Heynen, *Yves Klein*, 13.

11 Heynen, *Yves Klein*, 10.

12 Ibid., 16.

13 For a complete catalogue of the original furnishings, see Daniela Hammer-Tugendhat and Wolf Tegethoff, eds., *Ludwig Mies van der Rohe: Das Haus Tugendhat* (Vienna: Springer-Verlag, 1998), 144–61.

14 Grete Tugendhat, "The Inhabitants of the Tugendhat House give their Opinion," *Die Form: Zeitschrift für gestaltende Arbeit* 11 (November 1931): 437–38, as translated in Hammer-Tugendhat and Tegethoff, *Ludwig Mies van der Rohe: The Tugendhat House*, 35–37. Edith Fansworth's experiences with Mies and her house are the subject of Alice T. Friedman, "People Who Live in Glass Houses," in *Women and the Making of the Modern House*, 126–60.

15 Arthur Drexler, foreword to Tegethoff, *Mies van der Rohe: The Villas and Country Houses*, 9.

16 Gerhard Storck, foreword to Tegethoff, *Mies van der Rohe: The Villas and Country Houses*, 7.

17 Walter Cohen, "Haus Lange in Krefeld," 162.

18 Lange's role as patron of the landmark 1932 exhibition is in Jan Maruhn, "Building for Art: Mies van der Rohe as the Architect for Art Collectors" in Riley and Bergdoll, *Mies in Berlin*, 320.

19 Heynen, *Ein Ort der denkt/A Place That Thinks*, 25.

20 The image of Haus Lange appears in Yehuda E. Safran, *Mies van der Rohe* (Lisbon: Editorial Blau, 2000),

45. On page 39, Safran states that "Mies created some of his finest furniture designs for both houses, as can be seen in the layout of 1929–30." This assertion is augmented by the suggestion that the Barcelona chairs, despite being titled "*Pavillion Sessel*" were in fact designed for Haus Esters: "Pavilion Sessel, for the living room of Esters House."

21 Heynen, *Ein Ort für Kunst/A Place for Art*, 52. A slight variant occurs in Heynen, *Ein Ort der denkt/A Place That Thinks*, 33, and in Safran, *Mies van der Rohe*, 39.

22 This view is also featured in Wolf Tegethoff, "Museum Haus Lange und Haus Esters in Krefeld," *Baumeister* 9, (2000): 89.

23 Tegethoff, *Mies van der Rohe: The Villas and Country Houses*, 65.

24 Ibid., 65.

25 Peter Bürger, *Theory of the Avant-Garde*, trans. Michael Shaw (Minneapolis: University of Minnesota Press, 1984), 50.

LeWitt and the Art of Instructions

1 Barbara Reise, in an article on the drawings, states that the medium was silverpoint. See Barbara Reise, "Sol LeWitt Drawings 1968–69" in *Studio International* (December 1969): 222.

2 Sol LeWitt, "The Location of a Line" in *Sol LeWitt, Drawings 1958–1992* ed. Susanna Singer (The Hague: Haags Gemeentemuseum, 1992), project numbers 105 and 180.

3 Susanna Singer, ed., *Sol LeWitt, Wall Drawings 1968–1984* (Amsterdam: the Stedelijk Museum, 1984), 198.

4 In 1981, the instructions alone were exhibited at the Cranbrook Academy of Art Museum in a show aptly called Instruction Drawings. See Michael Hall, *Instructions Drawings: the Gilbert and Lila Silverman Collection* (Bloomfield Hills, Mich.: The Museum, 1981).

5 Sol LeWitt quoted in Rosalind E. Krauss, *The Originality of the Avant-Garde and Other Modernist Myths* (Cambridge, Mass: MIT Press, 1985), 254.

6 Ibid.

7 Singer, *Sol LeWitt, Wall Drawings 1958–1992*, project number 146.

8 Rosalind E. Krauss, *Passages in Modern Sculpture* (New York: Viking Press, 1977), 265–66.

9 Michael Fried, "Art and Objecthood" in *Art and Objecthood: Essays and Reviews* (Chicago: University of Chicago Press, 1998), 148–72.

10 Elsewhere, Fried acknowledges that "the concept of theatricality is crucial to my interpretation of French painting and criticism in the age of Diderot, and in general the reader who is familiar with my essays on abstract art will be struck by certain parallels between the ideas developed in those essays and in this book." See Michael Fried, *Absorption and Theatricality: Painting and the Beholder in the Age of Diderot* (Chicago: University of Chicago Press, 1980), 5.

11 Paul Wember, *Sol LeWitt Scultptures and Wall-Drawings* (Krefeld: Museum Haus Lange, 1969), unpaginated.

12 Sol LeWitt, "Excerpts from a Correspondence, 1981–1983," in Singer, *Sol LeWitt, Wall Drawings 1968–1984*, 23.

13 "*Es liegt uns gerade daran, die Bauerei von dem ästhetischen Spekulantentum zu befreien und Bauen wieder zu dem zu machen, was es allein sein sollte, nämlich BAUEN.*" Mies van der Rohe, *G Magazin* (September 1923) republished in Fritz Neumeyer, *The Artless Word: Mies van der Rohe on the Building Art*, trans. Mark Jarzombek (Cambridge, Mass.: MIT Press, 1991), 12, 14.

14 Mies van der Rohe, quoted in Reginald Malcomson, "The School of Mies van der Rohe: A Philosophy of Architectural Education" (Centennial Lecture, Illinois Institute of Technology, Chicago, 1986), 4.

15 Sol LeWitt, "Doing Wall Drawings" in *Sol LeWitt: Critical Texts*, ed. Adachiara Zevi (Rome: i Libri di Aeiuo, 1994), 95.

16 Blake, *Mies van der Rohe: Architecture and Structure*, 72.

17 Malcolmson, "The School of Mies van der Rohe," 2.

18 Evans, "Mies van der Rohe's Paradoxical Symmetries," 242–43.

19 Tegethoff, *Mies van der Rohe: The Villas and Country Houses*, 37, 42, and 43.

20 "*Der Grundriss des Backsteinhauses ist ein gutes Beispiel für die Art, wie Mies van der Rohe von allem Anfang an die Kunst der Struktur entwickelte. Die Struktur einer Backsteinwand beginnt schon bei der kleinsten teilbaren Einheit: dem Backstein.*" Werner Blaser, *Mies van der Rohe: Die Kunst der Struktur* (Zurich: Artemis Verlag, 1965), 20. Translation by the authors. Also quoted in a slightly different English translation in Tegethoff, *Mies van der Rohe: The Villlas and Country Houses*, 42.

21 The comparison between the plan of the Brick Country House and the paintings of van Doesburg began as early as 1936, in Alfred H. Barr Jr.'s *Cubism and Abstract Art*, a catalogue for the exhibition of the same name at the Museum of Modern Art in New York, wherein van Doesburg's *Rhythm of a Russian Dance* was reproduced next to the plan of the Brick Country House. See Detlef Mertins "Architectures of Becoming: Mies van der Rohe and the Avant-Garde" in Riley and Bergdoll, *Mies in Berlin*, 124. This tradition of comparison continued in Johnson, *Mies van der Rohe*, 30, as well as Schulze, *Mies van der Rohe: A Critical Biography*, 114–15. In the 1959 public interview with H. T. Cadbury-Brown at the Architectural Association in London, Mies spoke about the project:

> When I made this plan I made the drawings the night before the Exhibition. I made them the night before in charcoal so that people could see the drawings from a distance and did not have to read blueprints. It did not receive that interpretation in some quarters, but the interpretation placed upon it was nonsense. I just wanted to make it clear enough so that people could look at it.

See Cadbury-Brown, "Ludwig Mies van der Rohe: An Address of Appreciation," 30.

22 Frampton, *Studies in Tectonic Culture*, 167. Authors' italics.

23 Singer, *Sol LeWitt, Drawings 1958–1992*, project numbers 94, 95.

24 "*Lfd. No. 12: qm Verblendung der Umfassungswände als Zulage zum Mauerwerk des Kellergeschosses mit Bockhorner Klinkern, (Steinmasse 22/10, 5/5, 2) erste Sortierung, bunt, unter Weglassung der ganz blauen und der gelblichen Steine, 3 Schichten, unter Terrain beginnend, im Blockverband nach Zeichnung und Angabe, 16 Schichten auf 1 Meter mit dreimaliger Einbindung zu verblenden, die Fugen 1 cm tief auszukratzen und mit dem Besen abzufegen, einschl. Lieferung aller Materialien. Besonders zu beachten ist, dass die Brandkanten nach unten liegen.*" "Vereinbarte Preise für das Landhaus Hermann Lange, Krefeld" (Cost Estimate for the Hermann Lange House, Krefeld), Page 4, Folder 6, Item A, Mies van der Rohe Archive, Museum of Modern Art, New York. Translation by the authors.

25 "*Lfd. No. 6: cbm Mauerwerk der 63 cm strk. Wände des Kellergeschosses aus prima Ringofenziegelsteinen mit Kalkmörtel 1:6 in gutem Kreuzverband.*" Ibid., Page 3, Folder 6, Item A. Translation by the authors.

26 Ibid., Page 2, Folder 6, Item A.

27 Johnson, *Mies van der Rohe*, 35.

28 Dan Hoffman, "The Receding Horizon of Mies: Work of the Cranbrook Architecture Studio" in Mertins, *The Presence of Mies*, 102; Blake, *Mies van der Rohe: Architecture and Structure*, 38.

29 Measurements on site reveal a range of brick dimensions. On the course sampled, stretchers ranged from 21 cm to almost 22 cm in length, and headers from 10.1 cm to 10.7 cm. None of these variations are particularly egregious, nor are they unusually consistent, which is precisely the point: the ranges are, in fact, rather ordinary.

30 "[*U*]*nd wir halten es für notwendig, dass Sie sich die Wirkung einmal ansehen, umsomehr, als Herr Walther den ersten Waggon dieser Verblender sowohl wegen der ungleichen Masse der Steine als auch wegen der zu stark voneinander abweichenden Farben verworfen hatte.*" Letter from Josef Esters to Mies van der Rohe, 12 November 1928, Folder 3, Item B, Mies van der Rohe Archive, Museum of Modern Art, New York. Translation by the authors. It is most certain that the Herr Walther referred to here is the son of Ernst Walther, Sr., Mies's structural engineer. The younger Walther, also a structural engineer, worked periodically for Mies's office.

31 Neumeyer, *The Artless Word*, 316.

32 Sol LeWitt, "Doing Wall Drawings," in Zevi, *Sol LeWitt: Critical Texts*, 95.

33 Andrea Miller-Keller and Sol LeWitt in "Excerpts from a Correspondence, 1981–1983" in Zevi, *Sol LeWitt: Critical Texts*, 115.

34 Tegethoff's compelling analysis of the genesis of the Brick Country House project suggests that the scheme was intended for the architect himself and for a specific site. The title "*Grundriss zu einem Landhaus in Neubabelsberg*" ("Plan for a County House in Neubabelsberg") was discovered by Tegethoff on a negative of the plan. See Tegethoff, *Mies van der Rohe: The Villas and Country Houses*, 40–41 and specifically figure 3.2.

Serra and the Anti-Environment

1 Letter from Marianne Stockebrand to Clara Weyergraf and Richard Serra, November 28, 1983. Kaiser Wilhelm Museum Archive, Krefeld.

2 One piece not expressly made for the exhibition was *Plate Roll Prop* (1969), retitled *Corner Pole Prop* (1983), for the exhibition in Haus Lange. Letter from Alexander von Berswordt-Wallrabe to Dr. Gerhard Storck, November 23, 1984. Kaiser Wilhelm Museum Archive, Krefeld. For a photograph of the piece installed in the corner of the terrace, see Marianne Stockebrande, *Richard Serra* (Krefeld: Krefelder Kunstmuseum, 1985), 21.

3 Richard Serra, "Extended Notes from Sight Point Road," in *Writings, Interviews* (Chicago: University of Chicago Press, 1994), 171–72.

4 See Richard Serra, "Richard Serra's Urban Sculpture" in *Writings, Interviews*, 131.

5 Douglas Crimp, "Serra's Public Sculpture: Redefining Site Specificity" in Rosalind E. Krauss, *Richard Serra/Sculpture* (New York: Museum of Modern Art, 1986), 40–56.

6 Richard Serra, *Richard Serra: Weight and Measure 1992* (London: Tate Gallery Publications; Düsseldorf: Richter Verlag, 1992), 9.

7 Ibid., 11.

8 Ibid., 11.

9 Ibid., 13, 15.

10 Richard Serra, "Interview by Alfred Pacquement" and "Extended Notes from Sight Point Road," in *Writings, Interviews*, 164, 169. Stockebrand writes that Serra considered Mies one of "the most brilliant artists of the century." ("*. . . da [Serra] er Mies van der Rohe ohnehin zu den brilliantesten Künstlerpersönlichkeiten dieses Jahrhunderts zählt.*") See Stockebrand, *Richard Serra*, 14. Translation by the authors.

11 "*Am Haus Lange besticht immer wieder die Weitläufigkeit und Transparenz der offenen und ineinander übergehenden Raumbereiche. . . . Die riesigen Stahlplatten sind im Erdgeschoss von Haus Lange so postiert, dass die Weite der Räume eingeengt wird, der Raumfluss unterbrochen ist und die Durchblicke verstellt sind.*" Ibid. Translation by the authors.

12 "[W]hen Serra titles this intervention 'Two 45°-Angles for Mies' this is by no means without aggression or irony." Ulrich Reinke, "Kultur aktuell," *Südwestfunk Baden-Baden* (January 31, 1985). Translation by the authors.

13 Krefelder Kunstmuseen, *Richard Serra: Skulpturen und Zeichnungen*, promotional material (Krefeld, 16 January 1985), 1.

14 Author unknown, "Stählerne Raumschikanen," source unknown, Kaiser Wilheim Museum Archive, 3. ("*. . . umfassenden Praxis der verstörung.*") Translation by the authors.

15 Letter from Alexander von Berswordt-Wallrabe to Marianne Stockebrand and Gerhard Storck, March 15, 1985. Kaiser Wilhelm Museum Archive, Krefeld. Translation by the authors. The suggestion to keep the installation intact is in the same letter, page 1. It should be noted that as Serra's primary gallerist in Germany, Berswordt-Wallrabe may not have been entirely selfless in this suggestion.

16 Frampton, "Mies van der Rohe: Avant-Garde and Continuity," 167.

17 "For example, the structural calculations for my house, which are complete, comprise 124 fairly densely written pages. Approximately 50,000 kilo[grams] of steel were used in each of the two houses. I must confess that I had not imagined that the modern way of building. . . would result in such technical complications." (*Die statische Berechnung z.B. zu meinem Hause, die fertig ist, umfasst 124 ziemlich eng beschriebene Aktenseiten. In jedem der beiden Häuser werden etwa 50.000 Kilo Eisen verbraucht. . . . Ich muss gestehen, dass ich mir nicht vorgestellt hatte, dass sich durch die moderne Bauweise. . . solche technischen Komplikationen ergeben.*) Letter from Joseph Esters to Hermann Lange, 4 October 1928, Page 5, Folder 1, Item B, Mies van der Rohe Archive, Museum of Modern Art, New York. Translation by the authors.

18 The structural calculations for Haus Lange are in Folder 7, Item A, those for Haus Esters in Folder 8, Item A, Mies van der Rohe Archive, Museum of Modern Art, New York.

19 Columns 62–67.

20 Columns 34, 36, 37, and 38. Columns 36 and 37 rest above the living room.

21 Gombrich, "Art History and the Social Sciences," 164.

Windows and Other Weaknesses

1 Luke 10:38

2 Cadbury-Brown, "Ludwig Mies van der Rohe: An Address of Appreciation," 26–46.

3 Josef Esters to Hermann Lange, 4 October 1928, Folder 1, Item B, 6 pages, Mies van der Rohe Archive, Museum of Modern Art, New York.

4 "Yesterday we spoke with Mr. Hochkramer for the third time about the height of the sills of the south and

west windows." ("*Gestern haben wir mit Her Hochkramer zum dritten Mal wegen der Höho der Fenster-brüstung an den Süd- und Westfenstern gesprochen.*") Ibid., 2. Translation by the authors.

5 "*Ich muss gestehen, dass ich mir nicht vorgestellt hatte, dass sich durch die moderne Bauweise (Terrassen und grosse Fenster) solche technischen Komplikationen ergeben.*" Ibid., 5. Translation by the authors.

6 Turnovsky has written a small but brilliant pamphlet demonstrating Ludwig Wittgenstein's heroic and futile attempt to transfer geometric purity into material form in the design of his sister's villa in Vienna. See Jan Turnovsky, *Bauwelt Fundamente 77: Die Poetik eines Mauervorsprungs* (Braunschweig: Friedr. Vieweg & Sohn, 1987), 15.

7 Barry Bergdoll, "The Nature of Mies's Space" in Riley and Bergdoll, *Mies in Berlin*, 88–89.

8 For a brief discussion of Cartesian perspectivalism, as well as competing visual paradigms, see Martin Jay, "Scopic Regimes of Modernity," in *Vision and Visuality*, ed. Hal Foster, (Seattle: Bay Press, 1988), 3–23. Cartesian perspectivalism is summarized on page 15.

9 The principal text on the anamorphosis is Jurgis Baltrusaitis, *Anamorphic Art*, trans. Walter Strachan (New York: Harry N. Abrams, 1977).

10 Martin Jay contrasts the use of the flat mirror in analytic perspective to that of the curved mirror in the anamorphosis. The flat mirror played an important role in Brunelleschi's famous demonstration of the illusionistic power of linear perspective, where the image of the sky reflected in the mirror and the architecture of the painting merged seamlessly into one coherent image. In the anamorphosis, the image in the (curved) mirror is precisely not the same as the painted image; rather, the mirror effects a transformation and decoding of the painted image. See Jay, "Scopic Regimes of Modernity," 17.

11 Charles Baudelaire, "Windows," in *The Parisian Prowler: Le Spleen de Paris, Petits Poèmes en Prose*, trans. Edward K. Kaplan (Athens: University of Georgia Press, 1989), 93.

12 Victor I. Stoichita, *The Self-Aware Image: An Insight into Early Modern Meta-Painting*, (Cambridge: University of Cambridge Press, 1997), 3.

Conclusion: Architecture, Acting

1 Heynen, ed., *Ein Ort der denkt/A Place That Thinks*, 59 and 61.

2 Ibid, 63.

3 Fritz Tugendhat experienced his walls not as a substitute for art but as a fragment of a total artwork, the space of his villa: "The incomparable pattern of the marble, the natural grain of the wood, are not substitutes for art, but rather appear within the art, which is the sapce itself." "(*Die unvergleichliche Zeichnung des Marmors, die natürliche Masserung des Holzes sind nicht an die Stelle der Künst getreten, sie treten in der Kunst auf, im Raum, der heir Kunst ist.*") Fritz Tugendhat, "Kann man im Haus Tugendhat wohnen?" in *Die Form: Zeitschrift für gestaltende Arbeit* VI, 11 (November 1931): 437–38. Translation by the authors.

4 "[T]he Barcelona Pavilion distracts the entranced observer from what is troubling elsewhere. This is an architecture of forgetting." Evans, "Mies van der Rohe's Paradoxical Symmetries," 268.

5 Bertold Brecht, "Short Description of a New Technique of Acting which Produces an Alienation Effect," in *Brecht on Theatre: The Development of an Aesthetic*, ed. and trans. John Willett (New York: Hill and Wang, 1964), 136–47.

Appendix: Drawings

[1]   Site plan

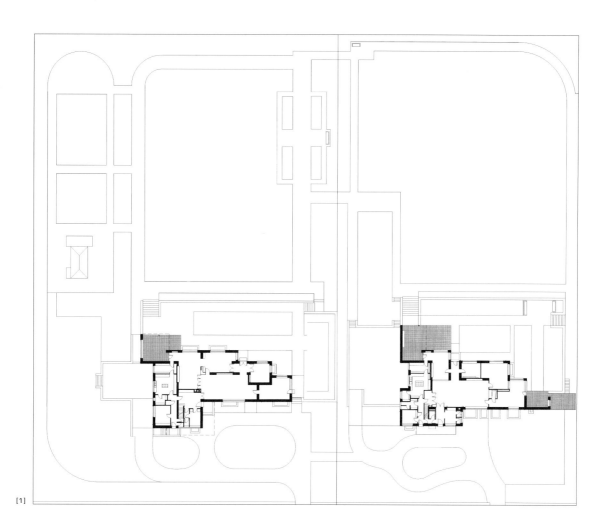

[1]

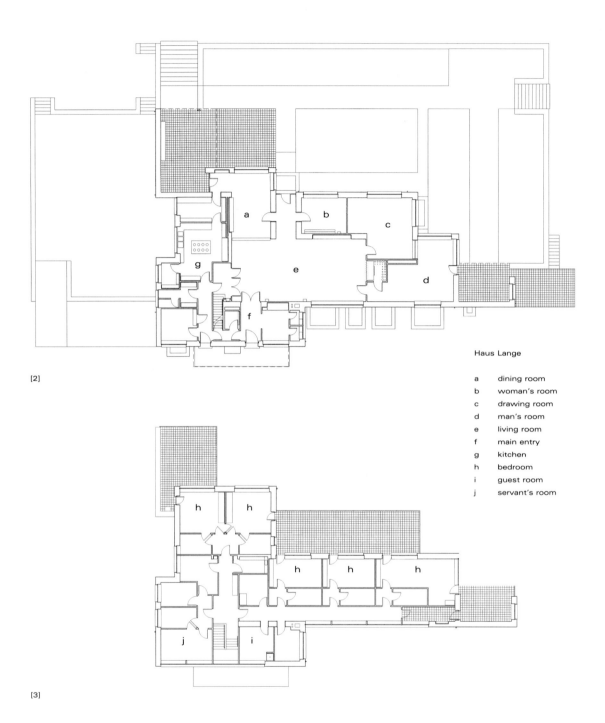

[2]

Haus Lange

a   dining room

b   woman's room

c   drawing room

d   man's room

e   living room

f   main entry

g   kitchen

h   bedroom

i   guest room

j   servant's room

[3]

[2]   Haus Lange, ground-floor plan

[3]   Haus Lange, upper-floor plan

[4]   Haus Esters, ground-floor plan

[5]   Haus Esters, upper-floor plan

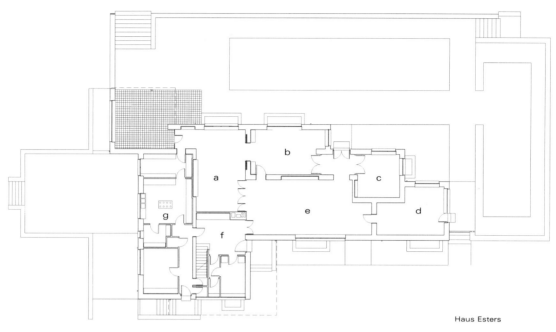

[4]

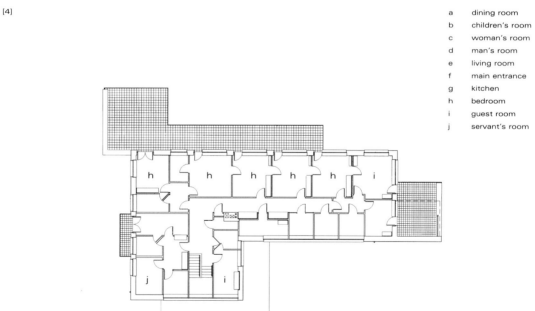

[5]

Haus Esters

a   dining room

b   children's room

c   woman's room

d   man's room

e   living room

f   main entrance

g   kitchen

h   bedroom

i   guest room

j   servant's room

[6]

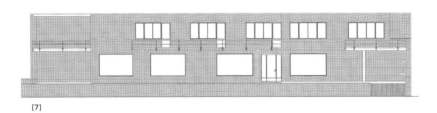

[7]

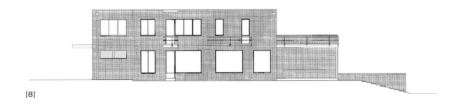

[8]

[9]

[6]   Haus Lange, north elevation
[7]   Haus Lange, south elevation
[8]   Haus Lange, west elevation
[9]   Haus Lange, east elevation
[10] Haus Esters, north elevation
[11] Haus Esters, south elevation
[12] Haus Esters, west elevation
[13] Haus Esters, east elevation

[10]

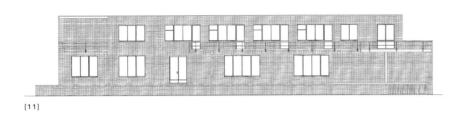

[11]

[12]

[13]

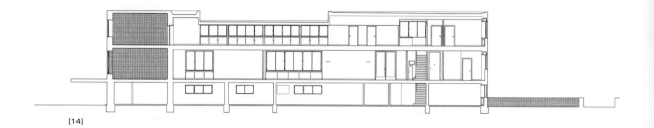

[14]

[15]

[14]   Haus Lange, longitudinal section

[15]   Haus Lange, cross section

[16]   Haus Esters, longitudinal section

[17]   Haus Esters, cross section

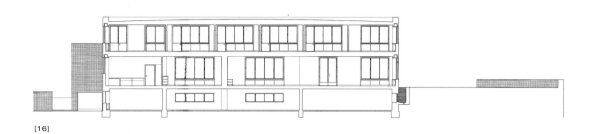

[16]

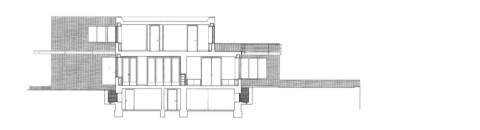

[17]

Credits